BRITISH
COMMERCIAL AIRCRAFT
sixty years in pictures

BRITISH COMMERCIAL AIRCRAFT
sixty years in pictures

Paul Ellis

JANE'S PUBLISHING COMPANY
LONDON · SYDNEY

For Nicky

Introduction

The development of commercial aircraft in Britain over the past sixty years has been a tortuous, sometimes haphazard journey taking designers and manufacturers down some extraordinary blind alleys in their search for the perfect aircraft with which to satisfy the conflicting desires of airline operator, pilot and passenger. While a good proportion of the resulting aircraft have been, at best, flawed by the necessity to compromise in one area or another and, at worst, ill-conceived, foolish and occasionally downright dangerous, many more have been notable successes in terms of aerodynamic efficiency, passenger safety and comfort, economy of operation, social acceptability or simple aesthetics. Seldom, however, have all these qualities been combined in a single aircraft.

Sadly, Britain's aircraft industry, lacking a substantial domestic market, will never enjoy the spectacular triumph of a Douglas DC-3 or Boeing 707. It can never on its own produce a rival to the Boeing, Lockheed and McDonnell Douglas wide-bodied commercial jets, and the business sector of general aviation will probably continue to be dominated in the years ahead by Beech, Piper and Cessna. Nevertheless, glancing back over the plentiful output of Britain's smaller industry during the last six decades, one can still recognise more than a handful of household names: the Avro 504s, Handley Pages and Armstrong Whitworth Argosies of the 1920s, and the de Havilland Hercules tri-motors, Handley Page H.P.42s, Dragon Rapides and Short Empire Flying Boats of the 1930s. Post-war milestones must include the Viscount, Comet and Britannia, while almost all of the more modern British commercial aircraft have achieved widespread recognition if not actual fame, as more and more ordinary people have benefited from the steady fall in air fares.

This healthy democracy in air travel is relatively recent, however, having grown up largely in the last fifteen years or so. When commercial aviation began in Britain, back in 1919, it was extremely expensive, often quite dangerous and frequently frustrated by unserviceability and the generally unpleasant north European weather. The aircraft were almost all war-surplus bombers—D.H.4s and Handley Page O/400s—hastily adapted for passenger-carrying by the provision of a cramped and draughty cabin containing a handful of wicker seats and precious little else in the way of comforts.

The parlous state of the British aircraft industry after the First World War—caused in part by the cancellation of hundreds of thousands of pounds' worth of contracts—meant that little money was available to finance serious development of future commercial aircraft. The result was that, up until the mid-1930s, the majority of British-built passenger-carrying aircraft were relatively simple biplanes embodying the design principles and construction techniques evolved during the war for long-range bombers.

British airlines and designers have been reproached for persisting with the biplane for so long after Continental airlines had, almost as soon as passenger services began, switched to monoplanes. However, analysis of comparable British and Continental designs shows that in the years up until about 1931 the massive British biplanes were not markedly inferior to their competitors and were in some respects even ahead of them.

The use of multi-engined aircraft for increased safety was a notable British contribution to commercial air travel, and Britain also set extremely high standards of passenger comfort, particularly aboard the types in service towards the end of that period, which were luxurious almost to the point of decadence. Nor was the performance of the British aircraft inferior to that of the European monoplanes; in fact the solidly reliable engines bolted to these biplane behemoths usually provided a top speed slightly higher than that of contemporary European types.

The first British commercial aircraft were converted wood-and-fabric biplane bombers. The first serious attempt to create a purpose-built airliner was the twin-engined Handley Page W.8, which first flew right at the end of 1919. Although it was an obvious development of the wartime Handley Page bombers, the W.8 was the first of a long line of multi-engined biplane aircraft which could justifiably claim the title "airliner".

Over the next few years the Handley Pages were followed into service by the tri-motor Armstrong Whitworth Argosy and de Havilland D.H.66 Hercules, which did so much to open up the Empire air routes in the late 1920s. There is something uniquely British in the spectacle of these superb anachronisms squatting on some sand-swept apron, determinedly resisting any possibilty of change or, God forbid, vulgar progress.

Probably the epitome of the deluxe biplane transport of the pre-war years was the elegant Handley Page H.P.42, which first entered service in 1931 on Empire and European routes. These extraordinary machines were still earning a living ten years later, when Heinkel and Dornier monoplane bombers, capable of more than 250 mph, were raining bombs on London. They flew more than ten million miles and established a safety and reliability record which few aircraft of the time could equal. Perhaps more important, they found a place in the heart of the British man in the street, who began to look on air travel not so much as an elitist pursuit but as a safe and socially useful means of traversing the globe.

The H.P.42 and the Short Scylla of 1934 were the last of the major biplane airliners, and henceforth British airlines turned with some reluctance to monoplanes to service their Empire routes. The biplane would however continue to find a place in the hangars of the smaller operators well into the 1950s.

First of the monoplane airliners was the delightfully chunky Armstrong Whitworth Atalanta. Thick-winged and solid, it had four radial engines almost buried in the generous wing leading edge. First flown in 1932, it could carry up to twenty passengers at a cruising speed of 125 mph.

During the late 1930s the long-range flying boat began to make its presence felt in British commercial aviation. Britain had a long history of flying boat development, particularly for military uses, but during the 1920s and early 1930s civil flying boats were something of a novelty, being used mostly in countries where the terrain or facilities did not favour the use of the conventional landplane. Leader in the field was undoubtedly Shorts, based at Rochester on the River Medway. This company's first serious attempt at a commercial flying boat was the S.8 Calcutta, first flown in 1928 for the Mediterranean section of Imperial Airways' route to India. This was followed by the larger Kent, with four engines against the Calcutta's three.

The major breakthrough came with the first of the Short S.23 Empire Flying Boats of the mid-1930s. Generally regarded as being ahead of its time, the Empire Boat was robbed of the rewards of a long commercial innings by the outbreak of the Second World War. Nevertheless, the Empires and their successors, the G-class boats of 1939, were extremely valuable during the war, when, along with a number of de-militarised Sunderlands, they were used by BOAC on several long-distance strategic routes.

For perhaps six or seven years after the Second World War most of the commercial aircraft on the longer routes were American-built to designs developed during the war years, when the British aircraft industry was principally devoted to the design and construction of military aircraft. During those years and for some time afterwards America was the only major power with resources to spare for non-military developments, and it was during that time that she established her unassailable lead in civil transport aircraft.

Even if the United Kingdom had not agreed to leave development of large transport aircraft to America, it is doubtful whether the British could have found the resources to be truly competitive. Money and raw materials were in short supply and industry was being run down after the hectic pace of the war years. Once again, Britain set about adapting military designs to serve as civil transports and the results were the spartan Lancastrian, Halton, Tudor and York. Never really intended for carrying passengers, they were cripplingly expensive to maintain and operate, their huge engines guzzling petrol at an alarming rate and their payloads restricted by fuselages suitable only for the carriage of bombs.

With the opening of the 1950s, however, came the first glimmerings of a new generation of purpose-built transports. The first two even moderately successful types were the Airspeed Ambassador and the Vickers Viking, both twin-engined aircraft. Neither was a particularly original or innovative design and only the small domestic market showed any real interest in them.

The first serious challenge to American supremacy came with the de Havilland Comet of the early 1950s. The Comet, an attractive swept-wing aircraft, was the first pure jet-driven airliner in the world. Offering three powerful inducements to large-scale air travel—comfort, quietness and speed—it seemed set fair for a long and profitable career. But de Havilland's vision of a world dominated by Ghost-powered Comets was rudely shattered by the loss of three examples during 1953 and 1954, resulting in the type's withdrawal from service until the cause—structural failure of the pressure cabin—had been pinpointed. The subsequent four-year delay before the type was re-introduced into service effectively cost Britain her slender lead in commercial jet aircraft development. This lead was in any case largely illusory, since the competing Boeing design, with its four podded engines, was technically more advanced than the Comet and possessed so much more growth potential than the British aircraft that the type is still in limited production for the military.

In addition to pure-jet aircraft, Britain also developed a number of turboprop types. In this limited field the UK almost certainly led the USA, although the rewards were generally pretty limited. Most successful of all the British turboprop aircraft was the Vickers Viscount series, large numbers of which are still in widespread use throughout the world. First flown in 1948, the Viscount did not enter service until 1953, partly because of the protracted development and certification programme and partly because of the now familiar phenomenon of airline interference, which manifests itself as a chronic inability to define a requirement accurately.

The Viscount demonstrated that turboprops offered substantial economy advantages, and this type of propulsion was subsequently used on a number of European aircraft and to a lesser extent on contemporary American types. Unfortunately, these advantages did not show up on long-haul types such as the Britannia. Although this excellent aircraft—nicknamed the "Whispering Giant" because of its low acoustic signature—was more economical to operate than the turbojets on the lucrative North Atlantic route, and although it had both the capacity and range to operate adequately and safely, it was doomed to an early retirement because passengers could make the crossing three or more hours more quickly in a Boeing 707 for the same price because fares were fixed by international treaty. Many passengers would have been glad to pay a substantially lower fare if the only penalty were a few more hours tacked on to the journey, but few were willing to travel more slowly for the same cost.

As for current types, it sometimes seems that British industry has done little more than go through the motions, building adequate aircraft with no more than the usual number of compromises, with the expected capacity or performance shortfalls, and at a price that reflects the upward spiral of costs.

Will Britain ever build another significant commercial aircraft? Regrettably, the answer is: probably not on its own and certainly nothing to equal the best of the past sixty years. With the exception of a handful of twin-engined third-level aircraft—a useful if limited product range—Britain currently has no major new commercial project in hand—unless you count the BAe 146, and few do. Were there to be a new edition of *British Commercial Aircraft* in, say, 1990, I wonder how many new types would be added to the present list?

D.H.4A G-EAMU was transferred from Instone Air Line to Imperial Airways in June 1924

de Havilland D.H.4

The D.H.4 was one of several First World War types to be converted for civil use at the end of hostilities. In addition to service with George Holt Thomas's pioneering Aircraft Transport and Travel, surplus D.H.4s also operated with SNETA, the fledgling Belgian airline. Unfortunately, the four aircraft supplied were destroyed either in crashes or in a hangar fire at Brussels in September 1921.

Other D.H.4s found their way to Canada, where they were used for forestry patrols by the Air Board Civil Operations Branch, and to Australia, where a few were used on a rudimentary airmail service.

The variant which saw most civil use in Britain was the D.H.4A, with its enclosed cabin seating two passengers face-to-face. This civilised innovation was introduced at the behest of Prime Minister Bonar Law, who had demanded a more comfortable vehicle for Cabinet Minis-

ters and their secretaries for the daily Peace Conference shuttle between Kenley and Paris. These early D.H.4As were operated by the RAF's No 2 (Communications) Squadron and were sold to Handley Page when the unit disbanded in 1919.

Nine civil D.H.4A modifications were produced, seven of which were on the British register. The other two went to SNETA and were destroyed in the Brussels hangar fire. The British machines fared only slightly better, with

two of their number suffering major crashes (G-EAHF in December 1919 and 'AVL in April 1921), while a third, G-EAHG, was forced down in the Channel in October 1919.

Operated by both Aircraft Transport and Travel and Handley Page, AT & T's aircraft ceased operations in 1920 when the company went into liquidation. The sole D.H.4A owned by Instone Air Line Ltd (G-EAMU *City of York*) survived to see the formation of Imperial Airways in April 1924.

G-EAMU in Instone Air Line livery and carrying the name *City of York* on the nose

D.H.9C G-EBUN, a SNETA conversion originally registered O-BELG.
It was sold to India as VT-AAL in January 1929

de Havilland D.H.9

The D.H.9 first flew in 1917 and
was designed as a successor to
the D.H.4, to which it bore a
more than passing resemb-
lance. This is not surprising,
since the prototype D.H.9 was
actually a converted D.H.4.

After the First World War civil
D.H.9s turned up in many
guises, being modified for training, mail carrying and, with particular success, as two-
passenger aircraft in the service
of Aircraft Transport and Travel
and Handley Page in Britain, and
KLM and SNETA in Europe.
D.H.9s found their way to
Australia and New Zealand,
India, Borneo and South America. So rugged and hard-wearing
was the type that some examples were still flying in more
remote areas well into the
1930s.

The D.H.9A, of which relatively few were built, was not
simply a conversion of the basic
D.H.9 airframe, as were the
other variants, but was an
entirely different aeroplane with
wings of increased span and
chord and a fuselage which featured a different method of construction. Thirteen were placed
on the British register, with one
subsequently being designated
D.H.9R (for racer). As with the
D.H.4, Imperial Gift D.H.9s were
supplied to Australia and Canada, the Canadian aircraft operating alongside the D.H.4s on
forestry patrols.

9

de Havilland D.H.16

The D.H.16, Airco's first purely civil type, was built up from D.H.9A components specifically for Aircraft Transport and Travel's Hounslow-Paris service. Only nine examples of this four-passenger biplane were built, the prototype making its maiden flight at Hendon in March 1919 and, bearing the temporary marking K-130, entering service with AT & T in May of that year.

Only one D.H.16 was sold abroad: G-EAQG, which went to Argentina for the Buenos Aires-Montevideo ferry service operated by the River Plate Aviation Co.

When AT & T ceased operations in 1920 its seven surviving D.H.16s were put into storage at Croydon (G-EACT, ex-K-130, having crashed in March 1920). All but two were broken up in 1922; the exceptions, G-EALM and 'APT, were put to work by the de Havilland Aeroplane Hire Service on an early-morning newspaper run between Lympne and Ostend. The two aircraft were later based at de Havilland's field at Stag Lane and offered for contract hire. In January 1923 G-EALM was destroyed in a crash during a test flight, killing the pilot. The surviving D.H.16, 'APT, was dismantled in the following July.

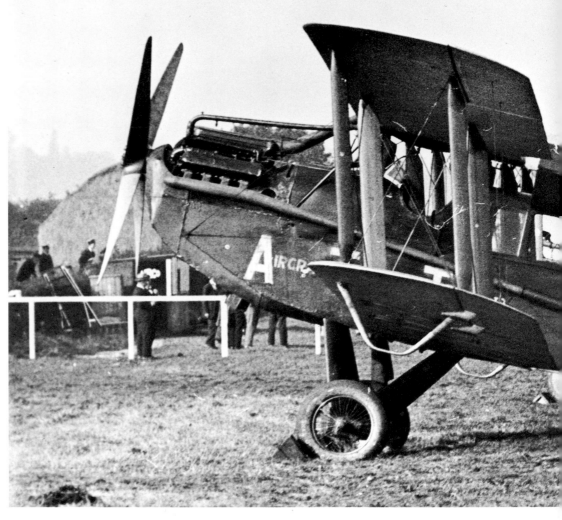

Seen here with his D.H.16 is AT & T pilot Capt Jerry Shaw

This D.H.16, G-EAQS, was operated briefly by
Aircraft Transport & Travel Ltd before being scrapped in 1922

G-EACT was originally registered K-130

11

Handley Page O/400

Another war-surplus type, the O/400 became a popular and moderately successful civil workhorse, carrying a dozen or more passengers. A total of 43 were converted for civil use, 34 of which were registered in Britain and operated in the colours of Handley Page Transport Ltd. First commercial flight was on May 1, 1919, when Lt Col W. F. Sholto Douglas (later Lord Douglas of Kirtleside) carried ten passengers from Cricklewood to Alexandra Park, Manchester.

Early O/400 conversions were makeshift affairs accommodating the passengers in a draughty, noisy fuselage lacking windows or any other creature comfort. But the introduction of the first O/7 version in August 1919 marked the beginning of a series of purpose-built aircraft which would one day merit the title "airliner". In the first nine months of operations Handley Page's nine O/400s and single O/7 carried 1,500 passengers and 40 tons of freight. By the end of 1920 the fleet included ten improved O/10s and three O/11s.

By the end of 1920 British airlines were floundering in the face of increasing competition from state-subsidised French carriers. HP Transport soldiered on until February 1921, when, like Aircraft Transport & Travel, it too ceased operations. A month later, however, operations were resumed on Croydon-Paris, with the British company offering a new subsidised fare of six guineas single or twelve pounds return, equal to the French carrier's rates.

H.P.12 G-EAAE *Vulture* **was a converted O/400 bomber**

G-EAAI, seen here at Hounslow in October 1919, was the prototype FK.26

BAT FK.26

Frederick Koolhoven's FK.26 was the first purely civil transport aircraft to be built in Britain after the First World War, flying for the first time at Hendon in April 1919. Built by the British Aerial Transport Co, this unusual-looking aircraft carried four passengers in a glazed cabin ahead of the pilot's open cockpit. The positioning of the pilot so far aft attracted a certain amount of criticism; Koolhoven is said to have replied by saying that while forward visibility might be reduced, the pilot's chances of surviving a crash (and explaining what had happened) would be greatly improved.

British Aerial Transport built four FK.26s, two of which were destroyed in crashes: G-EAHN in July 1920 and 'APK *City of Newcastle* in July 1922 while in the service of Instone Air Line. The remaining two were sold to Ogilvie Aircraft at Willesden in 1921 after BAT had closed down. Of these the prototype, 'AAI, was removed to Holland by the designer in 1937, while 'ANI was broken up in 1942, not having flown since passing into Ogilvie's ownership.

BAT FK.26 G-EAPK was sold to Instone Air Line in August 1920. It is seen here in company with D.H.16 G-EAQS

City of London **was operated for a while by Instone Air Line. It was transferred to Imperial Airways in 1924 and scrapped in 1926**

Vickers Vimy Commercial

The Vimy Commercial differed from demilitarised Vimy bombers in having a capacious new fuselage better suited to the carriage of freight and passengers. First flight of the prototype took place at Joyce Green in April 1919, the aircraft carrying the constructor's number K-107.

Although Vickers built a total of 43 Vimy Commercials between 1919 and 1922, only four carried British registrations. Almost all of the remainder were built for export to China. There they were intended for use on a mail service between Peking and Tsinan, but in the event few of the aircraft were even uncrated.

Best known of the Vimy Commercials was probably Instone's G-EASI *City of London*, which plied the Paris, Brussels and Cologne routes with almost clockwork precision in the early 1920s and is reported to have flown almost 108,000 miles by the time it was acquired by Imperial Airways in April 1924. It was eventually scrapped in 1926, although the cabin continued to serve as a summerhouse until destroyed by fire in 1935.

The 42nd and 43rd aircraft were both sold abroad: the first to French carrier Grands Express Aériens, registered F-ADER, and the second to Russia.

Vimy Commercial G-EAUL was one of several sold to China in 1921. It is seen here at Martlesham in August 1920

Avro 504M K-134, later G-EACX, made the first recorded British charter flights in 1919

Avro 504

The Avro 504 enjoyed a lengthy civil life which was no less distinguished than its military career. It is probably best remembered as a joyriding machine, and small armadas of this extraordinarily successful trainer roamed Britain, introducing many thousands of people to the new world of aviation. Most of these aircraft were 540Ks, modified to accommodate two passengers. Other more specialised versions included the float-equipped 504L, and the 504M, which boasted a rudimentary cabin for the pilot and two passengers.

To satisfy the demand for higher-capacity joyriding aircraft a number of Hamble-built 504Ks were given a nine-inch increase in width to allow four passengers to be carried in pairs in the rear cockpit. These hybrids were re-designated Avro 536 and re-engined with 150 hp Bentley BR.1s. Ten Hamble-built aircraft were joined later by a further 12 Manchester-built 536s and, during 1926 and 1927, by four more Clerget-engined aircraft built by Surrey Flying Services at Croydon.

G-EAIR was an Aircraft Transport & Travel Avro 504K

Kangaroo G-EAIU of North Sea Aerial & General Transport Co

Blackburn Kangaroo

This unlovely aircraft served originally as a long-range bomber, operating mainly from Seaton Carew in North Yorkshire on anti-submarine patrols during 1918. After the war ended the survivors of the 20 built were put up for sale by the Disposals Board. Three were acquired by the Grahame-White Aviation Co for joyriding, modifications being restricted to the removal of gun mountings and sufficient fabric from the top of the rear fuselage to allow seven passengers to be accommodated in two extremely crude cockpits. A further seven Kangaroos were bought by Blackburn subsidiary North Sea Aerial Navigation Co; two were equipped with a large glazed cabin seating seven passengers, with an eighth perched in the extreme nose.

The first of the two cabin aircraft, G-EAIT, and two open aircraft, G-EAIU and 'AKQ, were used by North Sea Aerial Navigation on a Leeds-Hounslow service which started on September 30, 1919. In early March 1920 the route was extended to Amsterdam, but the venture was not a success and 'AKQ was sold to the Peruvian Army Flying Service in July 1921.

G-EAMJ with open passenger cabin amidships

Bristol Tourer

Tourer was the generic name for a series of war-surplus Bristol Fighters fitted retrospectively with lower-powered engines and accommodation behind the pilot for one passenger or, in the case of those aircraft with a widened rear fuselage, two passengers side-by-side. Subsequently these aircraft had the Bristol type numbers 27, 28, 29 and 47 allotted to them.

Only two of the 28 aircraft in this series were delivered to UK operators. These were Type 47 G-EART, which S. Instone & Co used for charter work, and the privately owned Type 29, G-EAMB. Most of the remainder, which were Type 28s, went to Australia. Six were operated by West Australian Airways and one was used by Qantas and the Flying Doctor Service.

Two-seat Bristol 29 Tourer G-EAXA

The only Type 36 (Siddeley Puma), G-EAUE

D.H.18 G-EARI of Aircraft Transport & Travel

de Havilland D.H.18

The D.H.18 was the first Airco type to be designed specifically for airline operations. The prototype of this large single-engined biplane flew for the first time in early 1920, and in March of that year the aircraft went to Martlesham for trials.

Similar in configuration to the BAT FK.26, the D.H.18 was a little larger and accommodated up to eight passengers ahead of the pilot in his open cockpit. Only four D.H.18As were built, all serving initially with Aircraft Transport and Travel. The prototype, G-EARI, began operations on the Croydon-Paris route on April 8, 1920. This aircraft was wrecked after a forced landing at Wallington in August of that year and the remaining three were acquired by the Air Council following the collapse of AT & T in 1921. When state-subsidised air travel began in Britain in March 1921 the three aircraft were handed over to Instone Air Line. By the end of the year, however, Instone had lost two of its D.H.18s: G-EAUF *City of Paris* crashed in June and the certificate of airworthiness of 'ARO *City of Cardiff* expired in November. The Air Council supplied two replacement machines, designated D.H.18B and registered G-EAWW and 'AWX, which differed from the earlier aircraft in having plywood top decking over the rear fuselage and other detailed refinements.

With the recognition of Daimler Hire Service as an approved carrier Instone's remaining D.H.18A, 'AWO, was transferred to the new company for use on Croydon-Paris. This aircraft was lost in a mid-air collision with a Farman Goliath over Northern France on April 7, 1922, five days after operations began.

G-EARI eventually crashed at Wallington, Surrey, in August 1921

**Martinsyde Type A Mk 1
G-EAMR**

Martinsyde Type A

The Martinsyde series of civil aircraft were in the main derived from the F.4 single-seat fighter supplied to the RAF. The Type A Mk I long-range two-seater, G-EAMR, built in 1919 for the Australian Government's England-Australia prize flight, incorporated many F.4 components though the two-bay wings were of much greater span. This record attempt ended in tragedy when the aircraft ditched off Corfu on December 17, 1919, with the loss of both crew members.

Two of the other three Mk Is built were re-designated Type As and in July 1920 shipped to Quebec. There they were fitted with floats and used for timber survey and fire patrol work. The Type A Mk II was an improved version seating four passengers side-by-side in pairs in a glazed cabin located forward of the pilot, in the manner of the FK.26 and D.H.18. Four Mk IIs were built and all were exported, three to Canada and the fourth, christened *The Big Fella*, to the Irish Air Corps in June 1922. This particular aircraft is believed to be the fourth Mk I, G-EAPN, rebuilt to Mk II passenger-carrying standard.

Handley Page W.8

When the prototype W.8, G-EAPJ, flew for the first time on December 4, 1919, it was immediately clear that this purpose-built airliner was significantly superior to its war-surplus predecessors in both performance and economy. This was borne out by tests at Mart-lesham Heath in August 1920. Flown by Major Herbert Brackley, 'APJ won the highest award in the large-aeroplane class of the Air Ministry's comfort and safety competition. Handley Page Transport put this aircraft to work on the Croydon-Paris route on October 21, 1921.

Three 12-seat W.8bs were ordered by the Air Council in November 1921 and the first of these, G-EBBG *Bombay* (later named *Princess Mary*), was sent to Martlesham for trials in April 1922. The other two, 'BBH *Prince George* and 'BBI *Prince Henry*, joined Handley Page Transport in June. All three plied the Paris to Brussels routes until HPT was absorbed by Imperial Airways in April 1924. One other W.8b was built at Cricklewood; this was O-BAHK for Belgium's Sabena, joined later by three licence-built aircraft for use on the Amsterdam-Basle route.

Handley Page W.8 prototype G-EAPJ

G-EBBG was an improved W.8b

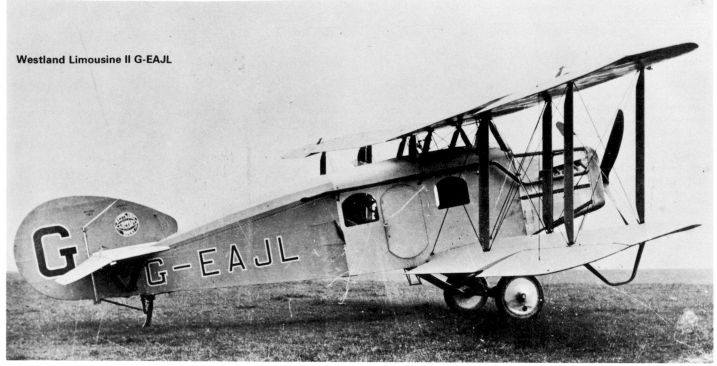

Westland Limousine II G-EAJL

Westland Limousine

This two-bay biplane was designed from the outset as a passenger-carrying commercial aircraft. The single Limousine I, G-EAFO, flew for the first time in July 1919. This aircraft was joined in October by the first of five Mk IIs, which differed from the prototype in having a fin and rudder of increased area and a new rectangular radiator for its Rolls-Royce Falcon.

'AFO and the first Mk II, 'AJL, were leased to Air Post of Banks Ltd for an experimental airmail service between Croydon and Le Bourget, but after two months both aircraft returned to the manufacturer's Yeovil base. Of the remaining Mk IIs, two ('ARE and 'ARF) were used by Instone Air Line on the Paris and Brussels routes.

Larger than the Mk IIs were the two Lion-engined Mk IIIs, G-EARV and 'AWF. While earlier aircraft could accommodate three passengers, the improved three-bay Mk III was designed to carry five passengers in addition to the single pilot. Service life of these early commercial aircraft was frequently very short: Instone's only Mk III ('AWF) and its Mk IIs lasted only until 1923, when they were scrapped at Croydon. The remaining Limousines all eventually found their way to Canada, where they were used by the Aerial Survey Company of Newfoundland until the end of 1923.

G-EARV was one of only two Limousine IIIs built

Vickers Viking Amphibian

The name Viking was applied to a series of four marks of amphibian, each of which differed significantly from the others in weight, dimensions and performance. The only Viking I to be built, G-EAOV, flew for the first time at Brooklands in October 1919. On December 18 it crashed near Rouen, killing the pilot, Sir John Alcock.

Viking II G-EASC, powered by a 360 hp Rolls-Royce Eagle VIII, won first prize in the Antwerp seaplane trials in August 1920. This variant was superseded by Mk III 'AUK, powered by a 450 hp Napier Lion. Itself a winner, 'AUK carried off the first prize of £10,000 in the amphibian competition held by the Air Ministry at Martlesham Heath in September 1920. This Mk III was effectively the prototype for the main production version, the Mk IV, of which 28 were built.

The most important of the small number of Viking operators was the River Plate Aviation Co, which used two Mk IVs on its Buenos Aires-Montevideo ferry service. But despite the popularity of this service it was not a commercial success, and when the Argentinian Government withdrew its financial support the aircraft were taken out of service.

Two views of Viking III G-EAUK

Bristol Ten-Seater

The British Treasury decision in early 1921 to subsidise approved air carriers resulted in a small though significant increase in the number of specialised commercial aircraft designed and built by British manufacturers. Frank Barnwell, of the Bristol Aeroplane Company, was encouraged by this development to begin work on a Napier Lion-engined biplane to carry nine passengers and one pilot. Registered G-EAWY, the Bristol Type 62 flew for the first time in June 1921. It was put into experimental service the following month but was not handed over to its intended user, Instone Air Line, until June 1922. Later it was loaned for a time to Handley Page Transport for that company's London-Cologne cargo service.

A developed version, powered by the 425 hp Bristol Jupiter IV radial engine and designated Type 75, flew for the first time in July 1922. Registered G-EBEV and fitted out for eight passengers and a crew of two, the new Ten-Seater was bought by Instone in February 1924. By the time it had received its full certificate of airworthiness, however, Instone and the three other state-subsidised carriers had been merged to form Imperial Airways, which used the Type 75 as a pure freighter on London-Cologne from July 1924. It was withdrawn from service in 1926.

G-EAWY was the Bristol Type 62 Ten-Seater . . .

. . . and G-EBEV was the Type 75 Ten-Seater

Line-up of Instone Air Line D.H.34s in March 1934

A Daimler Hire Ltd D.H.34

de Havilland D.H.34

The nine-passenger D.H.34 was developed to take advantage of the steadily increasing volume of cross-Channel traffic which resulted from the British Treasury's 1921 subsidy of approved air carriers. A direct descendant of the D.H.18 and the monoplane D.H.29, the Napier Lion-engined D.H.34 was a two-bay biplane carrying a crew of two in an open cockpit ahead of a glazed passenger cabin.

Daimler Hire Co ordered two of the type, the first of which, G-EBBQ, flew for the first time at Stag Lane in March 1922. A total of 12 were built, one of which, the seventh machine built and first flown in June 1922, was ordered by the Russian airline Dobrolet. A total of six D.H.34s went to Daimler which suffered a distressingly high loss rate with the type: 'BBU crashed at Berck, northern France, in

November 1922, and in the following August the prototype also crashed at Berck. September witnessed the loss of 'BBS, which crashed at Ivinghoe Beacon in Bedfordshire, killing the crew of two and three passengers. Last of the Daimler aircraft to crash was 'BBX, which was destroyed shortly after take-off from Croydon in December 1924, with the loss of the pilot and seven passengers.

Instone, which took delivery of four D.H.34s, fared only a little better, losing 'BBR *City of Glasgow* in May 1924, a month after the Imperial Airways merger.

Imperial Airways maintained its seven D.H.34s in regular service on the Brussels and Amsterdam routes until 1926, withdrawing them at the end of the financial year on March 31 after deciding to re-equip with multi-engined aircraft.

Vickers Vulcan

A spectacularly ugly aeroplane, the Vulcan was nevertheless a worthy attempt to build an aircraft which would pay its way without government subsidy. The fuselage was similar to that of the Vimy Commercial, with space for eight passengers and their baggage, and the single-bay wings were attached directly to the fuselage top and bottom. Sitting in lordly splendour in front of the upper mainplane, the pilot had a magnificent view interrupted only by the two-blade propeller attached to the 360 hp Rolls-Royce Eagle which towed the whole contraption through the air at around 90 mph.

Unfortunately for Vickers the Vulcan was not destined to achieve the results which designer Rex Pierson had hoped for: directional instability, a power deficiency and the meagre top speed each contributed to the several mishaps suffered by the type during its career. Vulcan G-EBET, delivered to Qantas in late 1922, was returned to Britain after tests had highlighted the type's inadequate performance. Despite this setback, construction of eight more Vulcans was begun at Brooklands; the first of these, 'BDH and 'BEA, joined the prototype at Croydon in the service of Instone Air Line. Promptly dubbed the "Flying Pigs", the three Vulcans were used chiefly on the Brussels route.

The final pair to be built, 'BFC and 'BLB, were fitted with the more powerful Napier Lion and operated at higher all-up weights. They were used on Imperial Airways' Continental services, 'BFC being withdrawn from service in 1926 and 'BLB remaining in use until destroyed in a fatal crash in July 1928.

Vulcan G-EBLB at Croydon in August 1926

Imperial Airways Vulcan G-EBFC at Croydon

de Havilland D.H.50

Designed as a direct replacement for the de Havilland Hire Service D.H.9Cs, the D.H.50 could carry three passengers in addition to the pilot. The prototype, G-EBFN *Galatea*, flew for the first time at Stag Lane on July 30, 1923, with Hubert Broad at the controls. Four days later Alan Cobham flew it to the International Aeronautical Exhibition at Gothenburg, where, in competition with the premier European commercial aircraft of the day, it romped home with 999 points out of a possible 1,000 to win first prize in the reliability trials. *Galatea* was acquired by West Australian Airways at Perth, Western Australia, in February and re-registered G-AUEY; it was withdrawn from service in April 1935.

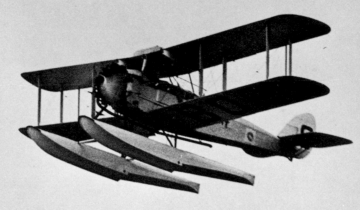

Pelican **was operated by**
North Sea Aerial & General Transport Co

A total of 38 D.H.50s were built, 17 by de Havilland at Stag Lane and the balance by manufacturers in Australia, Belgium and Czechoslovakia. Of the eight British-registered aircraft, two served with Imperial Airways: 'BFP, which was eventually disposed of to the Iraq Petroleum Transport Co in 1932, and 'BKZ, the slightly modified D.H.50A, which was destroyed in October 1928.

D.H.50s were fitted with a variety of engines, ranging from the 230 hp Siddeley Puma of the prototype to the 450 hp Pratt & Whitney Wasp C; weights and performances were equally varied. The D.H.50 was well-liked by pilots and operators and demonstrated quite remarkable longevity for a wood-and-fabric design, at least one Australian example surviving into the 1940s.

Vickers Vanguard

The one and only Vanguard built, G-EBCP, was a developed version of the Victoria military transport, with a widened cabin to accommodate 22 passengers in addition to the crew of two. It flew for the first time on July 18, 1923, with Stan Cockerell at the controls and was powered at that time by two 450 hp Napier Lions. Although the Vanguard proved pleasant to handle it was decided to re-engine the aircraft with more powerful Rolls-Royce Condor IIIs to improve performance. This was carried out in

1925, along with minor airframe modifications.

Imperial Airways did not take possession of 'BCP until May 1928, when it was put to work on the London to Paris route. After a short time the Vanguard was switched to the London-Brussels-Cologne service, remaining on that route until it was returned to Brooklands in October for modifications. The Vanguard was destroyed in May 1929 in a crash that resulted in the death of test pilot E. R. C. "Tiny" Scholefield.

G-EBCP was the only Vanguard

D.H.50A G-EBOP *Pelican*

G-EBCP at Weybridge

W.9 Hampstead G-EBLE

G-EBLE of Imperial Airways in October 1925

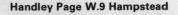

Handley Page W.9 Hampstead

In 1924 Handley Page at Cricklewood developed a three-engined version of the W.8 for Belgian airline Sabena. This model had a 360 hp Rolls-Royce Eagle IX in the nose and a pair of 240 hp Siddeley Pumas in wing nacelles. Designated the W.8e, this awkward-looking aeroplane was registered O-BAHG and was joined by eight more Sabca-built aircraft in 1925 for the Belgian airline's Congo service and a further two for European routes.

At much the same time the Air Ministry in Britain ordered another three-engined prototype for operational trials on the London-Paris-Zurich route. This was designated W.8f Hamilton and flew for the first time in June 1924. Registered G-EBIX and named *City of Washington*, it was used by Imperial Airways on the European route for some years. Converted to W.8g standard in early 1930, it crashed at Neufchatel, France, in October of that year.

Further three-engined development work led to the W.9 Hampstead, similar to the W.8e and W.8f but powered by three 385 hp Armstrong Siddeley Jaguar IV engines. The single example to be built, G-EBLE, flew for the first time on October 1, 1925. Named *City of New York*, it entered service with Imperial Airways on London-Paris on November 3; in the following March the Jaguars were replaced by Bristol Jupiters.

In March 1929 'BLE was declared surplus to the airline's requirements and was crated up for shipment to Port Moresby, New Guinea, where it was to be used by New Guinea Goldfields Ltd. For several months the W.9 ferried cargo between Wau and Salamaua, over an 8,000ft mountain range, until on May 30, 1930, the pilot lost control in thick cloud and the aircraft crashed. Miraculously, both crew survived.

de Havilland D.H.54 Highclere

The single-engined Highclere, a logical development of the D.H.34, might have been a perfectly useful passenger-carrying aircraft, with a capacity of twelve, had not Imperial Airways decided on a policy of using only multi-engined types on its passenger routes.

Larger than the D.H.34 and weighing around 4,000lb more, the Highclere carried its upper mainplane on centre-section struts and had dihedral on the lower wings only. A crew of two was carried in an open cockpit ahead of the wings, and its 650 hp Rolls-Royce Condor IIIA gave a top speed of around 110 mph. The prototype (and only example built), G-EBKI, flew for the first time at Stag Lane on May 28, 1925, with Hubert Broad at the controls.

Trials at Martlesham Heath were completed by March 1926 and a full certificate of airworthiness was granted. The Imperial Airways ruling on single-engined aircraft resulted in a reappraisal of the aircraft and, after some test flying at Farnborough, it was sent in November 1926 to Croydon for service on the airline's freight routes. The Highclere did little flying, however, and came to an abrupt end in February 1927 when a hangar collapsed on top of it.

The only D.H.54 Highclere, G-EBKI

Handley Page W.10

The twin-engined W.10, essentially an improved version of the W.8, was built in response to an urgent call from Imperial Airways for more multi-engined aircraft for its European service. Striving to meet a delivery deadline of March 31, 1926, Handley Page saved precious time by grafting a W.8 front fuselage to an existing military Hyderabad airframe, the new aircraft being powered by a pair of 450 hp Napier Lions fitted with long exhaust pipes to reduce cabin noise.

Four of these 14-passenger aircraft were built and all were certificated in March 1926. Registered G-EBMM, 'BMR, 'BMS and 'BMT, they carried the class names *City of Melbourne*, *City of Pretoria*, *City of London* and *City of Ottawa*. First into service was 'BMR, which was joined by the other three in time for duty during the General Strike. Disaster soon followed, however, with 'BMS *City of London* ditching in the Channel on October 21, 1926, though with no loss of life. First fatal accident was the loss of 'BMT *City of Ottawa* in the Channel on June 17, 1929, when four passengers were drowned.

In 1933 the two surviving aircraft were sold to Alan Cobham. 'BMM was renamed *Youth of New Zealand* and converted to a tanker for the refuelling of Cobham's Airspeed Courier at the start of his 1934 non-stop flight to India. It was destroyed in a fatal crash in September 1934. Only 'BMR *City of Pretoria* survived, finally being scrapped in Malta.

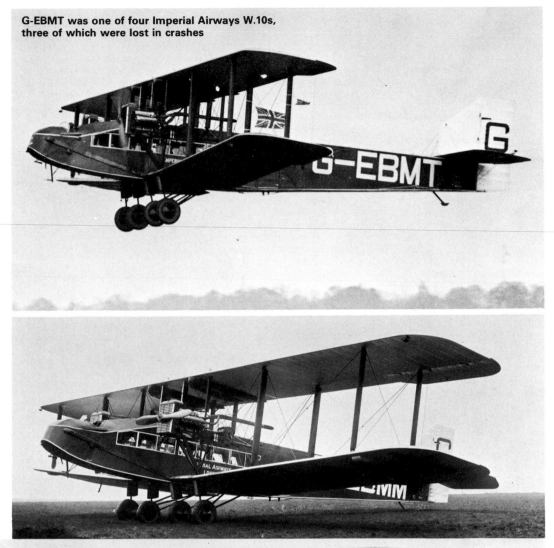

G-EBMT was one of four Imperial Airways W.10s, three of which were lost in crashes

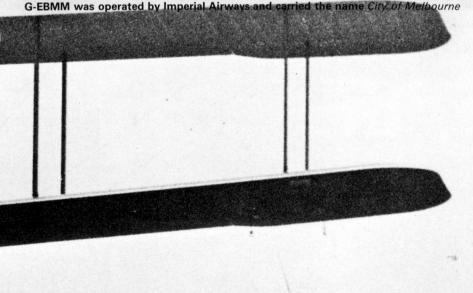

G-EBMM was operated by Imperial Airways and carried the name *City of Melbourne*

Armstrong Whitworth Argosy

The three-engined Argosy was the largest British airliner when it flew for the first time on March 16, 1926. With accommodation for 20 passengers in its capacious flat-sided cabin, it was the first Imperial Airways aircraft to provide anything like Pullman luxury, although the Handley Pages had come close, and gave an excellent account of itself on the London-Paris "Silver Wings" lunchtime service.

Three Argosies were built originally: G-EBLF *City of Glasgow*, 'BLO *City of Birmingham* and 'BOZ *City of Wellington* (renamed *City of Arundel*). Powered by three direct-drive Armstrong Siddeley Jaguar IIIs, they were not significantly better than comtemporary aircraft, with a cruising speed of only 90 mph and a maximum range of

405 miles. But they were much cheaper to operate, returning a cost per ton-mile practically half that of the W.10. Imperial Airways showed its satisfaction by ordering four improved Argosies in 1928. The Mk II aircraft had the more powerful geared Jaguar IVAs and, with greater fuel capacity, offered longer range. Registered G-AACH, 'ACI, 'ACJ and 'AEJ, they carried the names *City of Edinburgh*, *Liverpool*, *Manchester* and *Coventry* respectively.

The introduction of the Mk IIs more or less coincided with the opening up of the Imperial Airways Empire routes, which for the first time would take air travel outside the confines of Europe. Thus on March 30, 1929, the first London-Karachi airmail service was inaugurated by *City*

of Glasgow. The initial problems were enormous, and there were regular long delays as a result of accidents, unserviceability and shortage of aircraft. Nevertheless, the Argosy was a well liked and useful aircraft, seeing service in many parts of the Empire. Though three of the seven were destroyed in accidents, only one of these resulted in fatalities, when 'ACI *City of Liverpool* caught fire in mid-air over Belgium on March 28, 1933, killing three crew and twelve passengers.

Seen here at Croydon in March 1929 is the first Argosy I, G-EBLF

G-AACH *City of Edinburgh* **was one of four Argosy IIs**

G-EBLO was the second of three Argosy Is

ANEC III

The three ANEC IIIs, which never in fact saw service in Britain, were built under a contract originally placed by the Larkin Aircraft Supply Co with the Handasyde Aircraft Co and later transferred to the Air Navigation and Engineering Co Ltd.

First flown on March 23, 1926, the prototype ANEC III bore a superficial resemblance to the D.H.34, with the pilot in an open cockpit ahead of the wings and the six passengers accommodated in a glazed cabin. Registered G-AUEZ, 'UFC and 'UGF and named *Diamond Bird, Satin*

Bird and *Love Bird* respectively, the three aircraft went into service with a Larkin subsidiary, Australian Aerial Services.

Diamond Bird and *Love Bird* were withdrawn from service at the end of 1928 and were rebuilt as eleven-seaters and re-named Larkin Lascowls. The opportunity was also taken to re-engine both aircraft with 485 hp Armstrong Siddeley Jaguar supercharged radials. Re-registered VH-UEZ and 'UGF, the two Lascowls plied the Camooweal and Daly Waters route from February 19, 1930.

Handley Page Hamlet

The Handley Page Hamlet was built to Air Ministry Specification 23/24, which called for a six or seven-seat air taxi or charter aircraft powered by three engines totalling 400 hp. Originally powered by three 120 hp Bristol Lucifer IV three-cylinder radials, it was furnished in "executive" layout, accommodating only four passengers in addition to the crew of two. Registered G-EBNS, the Hamlet flew for the first time on October 19, 1926. However, it was found that the nose-mounted power-plant vibrated excessively, and it was decided to replace the Lucifers with 150 hp Armstrong Siddeley Mongoose five-cylinder engines. These were not immediately available and a pair of 220 hp Armstrong Siddeley Lynxes were installed temporarily, the nose station being blanked off with a curved fairing.

The three Mongoose engines finally became available in September 1927, but they were not fitted until the following March. The Hamlet never flew again and after delivery by road to the Royal Aircraft Establishment at Farnborough it was eventually scrapped there in 1929, a sad fate for an attractive and potentially successful aircraft.

H.P.32 Hamlet G-EBNS with Lynx engines

de Havilland D.H.66 Hercules

The D.H.66 Hercules was one of the classic airliners of the late 1920s and early 1930s. Originally designed for Imperial Airways' Cairo-Karachi passenger and mail route, the three-engined seven-passenger Hercules would later be found operating as far away as Australia.

The prototype, G-EBMW, was flown for the first time by Hubert Broad at Stag Lane on September 30, 1926, and after acceptance trials it left for Cairo on December 18. The five aircraft called for in the original contract were delivered between December 1926 and the following spring; they were 'BMW *City of Cairo*, 'BMX *City of Delhi*, 'BMY *City of Baghdad*, 'BMZ *City of Jerusalem* and 'BNA *City of Teheran*.

In 1928 West Australian Airways selected the Hercules for its new Perth-Adelaide passenger and mail service. The contract called for four aircraft modified to include an enclosed cabin for the crew and seating for 14 passengers. These aircraft, G-AUJO, 'UJP, 'UJQ and 'UJR, were built at Stag Lane and shipped to Perth, Western Australia, in the spring of 1929.

Imperial Airways ordered a sixth Hercules, G-AAJH *City of Basra*, in 1929 when its Cairo-Karachi route was extended to Delhi. This aircraft was fitted with the enclosed cockpit of the Australian order, and all of the original Imperial Airways machines were later modified in this way. In September 1929 *City of Jerusalem* was destroyed in a fatal crash at Jask, Persia, and Imperial Airways ordered its seventh and final Hercules, 'ARY *City of Karachi*, which was commissioned at Heliopolis in February 1930. When *City of Teheran* was damaged beyond repair at Gaza on February 14 the British airline approached West Australian Airways and negotiated the purchase of 'UJR, which was re-registered G-ABCP *City of Jodhpur* in July of that year. A second Australian aircraft, 'UJQ, was added to the Imperial Airways inventory after the loss of the prototype on April 19, 1931, during an experimental Croydon-Melbourne mail service. The replacement was re-registered G-ABMT and named *City of Cape Town*.

Prototype D.H.66 G-EMBW

The second D.H.66, G-EBMX, in Imperial Airways livery

D.H.66 with enclosed pilot's cockpit.

Unmarked D.H.66 at Stag Lane

de Havilland D.H.61 Giant Moth

The Jupiter-powered D.H.61 Giant Moth was built originally to meet an Australian requirement for a D.H.50 replacement. Like the D.H.50 it was a two-bay biplane with the pilot set well aft of the glazed passenger cabin, which could accommodate six to eight people, depending on the amount of baggage carried.

First flight of the prototype, G-EBTL, was made by Hubert Broad at Stag Lane in December 1927. After flight trials the aircraft was shipped to Melbourne in the following February. Originally named *Canberra*, it was christened *Old Gold* by its new owner, MacRobertson Miller Aviation Co.

Some ten Giant Moths were built, of which two plus the prototype were registered in Britain. One of the aircraft was G-AAAN, bought by the *Daily Mail* in August 1928 and used as a mobile newspaper office for 18 months before passing to National Flying Services, which used it for joyriding. In 1932 G-AAAN was flown out to New Guinea and re-registered VH-UQJ. The third British-registered D.H.61 was 'AEV *Youth of Britain*, which was bought by Alan Cobham Aviation. At the end of the 1929 tour Cobham sold 'AEV to Imperial Airways and delivered it himself to Salisbury, Rhodesia, where it was wrecked in a crash at Broken Hill on January 19, 1930.

Two Giant Moths were fitted with floats and delivered to Western Canada Airways and the Ontario Provincial Air Service, which used them to carry fire crews to forest outbreaks. They were registered G-CAJT and 'APG and were joined the following year by 'ARD. The last-named was never used and it is believed that its components were incorporated into the Canadian-built CF-OAK, which flew for the first time in June 1932, powered by a 525 hp Pratt & Whitney Hornet.

The other three D.H.61s were Australian-registered and used mainly on airmail work: G-AUHW by Larkin's Australian Aerial Services and 'UJB and 'UJC by Qantas.

D.H.61 Giant Moth G-AAEV of the Alan Cobham Aviation Co

de Havilland D.H.75 Hawk Moth

The high-wing, single-engined Hawk Moth was flown for the first time at Stag Lane by Hubert Broad on December 7, 1928, powered by Major Halford's 198 hp D. H. Ghost V8 engine. The prototype, G-EBVV, was found to be underpowered and production aircraft were accordingly fitted with the more powerful Armstrong Siddeley Lynx and larger wings. They were designated D.H.75A.

Following demonstrations in Canada by G-AAFW an order for three was received from the Canadian Government in 1930. These were CF-CCA (ex-G-AAFW), G-CYVL and 'YVM. In Australia G-AAFX was used by de Havilland Aircraft Pty Ltd as a demonstrator and later as an air taxi by Hart Aircraft Services of Melbourne.

The Hawk Moth was one of de Havilland's less commercially successful aeroplanes and production was suspended after only eight had been built, the main reason cited being competition from similarly configured but higher-powered American types.

Prototype D.H.75 Hawk Moth G-EBVV

Short Calcutta

Short's metal-hulled Calcutta was essentially a development of the RAF's Singapore, with three engines instead of two, slightly greater wing area and a deeper, wider hull. The two pilots were accommodated side-by-side in an open cockpit ahead of a cabin furnished for 15 passengers, with a steward's seat, galley and washroom aft. This roomy and comfortable machine was quite luxuriously appointed by the standards of the day.

The prototype, G-EBVG, flew for the first time on February 21, 1928, from the Medway at Short's Rochester works, with J. Lankester Parker at the controls. In mid-March the Calcutta was flown from Rochester to the MAEE at Felixstowe for airworthiness and sea handling trials and later, during August, to Westminster to be inspected by members of the Houses of Parliament.

Imperial Airways took possession of 'BVG *City of Alexandria* on August 9 and immediately began crew training. The second Calcutta, 'BVH *City of Stonehaven*, had meanwhile made its first flight. Later in the summer 'BVH joined *City of Alexandria* on a number of scheduled flights between Southampton and the Channel Islands, this service continuing until February 1929. The third Calcutta flew in April, at much the same time as Imperial Airways was beginning its new Mediterranean route from Genoa to Alexandria. The new aircraft, G-AADN *City of Rome*, flew the route with the two original aircraft until it was forced down off Spezia in a gale and foundered with the loss of the three crew and four passengers.

The Breguet Company's Calcutta, F-AJDB

Four other Calcuttas were built, two of them for Imperial Airways and the other two for France (F-AJDB going to aircraft manufacturer Breguet and the other to the French Navy). G-AASJ *City of Khartoum* was used on the Khartoum-Kisumu section of the Empire route until it crashed, out of fuel, off Alexandria on New Year's Eve 1935. The pilot, Capt V. G. Wilson, escaped but 12 of his passengers were killed. Calcutta 'ATZ *City of Salonika* (later *City of Swanage*) was ordered as a replacement for *City of Rome*. 'ATZ was transferred to Air Pilots Training Ltd at Hamble in October 1937 and scrapped in 1937.

Calcutta G-EBVH *City of Athens*, **operated by Imperial Airways**

Prototype Calcutta G-EBVG

Westland Wessex

The three-engined Westland IV was designed primarily as a taxi or feederliner, carrying a crew of two and four passengers. The prototype, G-EBXK, flew for the first time at Yeovil on February 22, 1929. A second aircraft, with 105 hp Hermes I engines replacing the 95 hp Cirrus IIIs of 'BXK, first flew in the following summer, being operated later by the private-hire division of Imperial Airways at Croydon. Two other Mk IVs were begun, G-AULF for Shell in Australia and G-AAJI for Wilson Airways in Nairobi, but these orders fell through and Westland took the opportunity to complete 'AJI with 105 hp Armstrong Siddeley Genet Major radials. This aircraft then became the prototype Wessex, carrying the new registration G-ABAJ. First flight of this aircraft took place in May 1930, after which, together with G-AULF, it was supplied to Sabena as part of an order for four machines for the Belgian airliner's shorter Continental services. The four Belgian aircraft were registered OO-AGC, 'AGD, 'AGE and 'AGF.

The next Wessex to be built was the Genet Major Ia-powered G-ABEG, which, after a brief career as a charter aircraft, was acquired by Imperial Airways, together with another higher-powered Wessex, 'CHI, in the summer of 1933. Two other Wessexes were built: 'BVB for the Portsmouth, Southsea and Isle of Wight Aviation Co for its Portsmouth-Ryde and Shoreham-Portsmouth runs; and 'CIJ, which was supplied to the Egyptian Air Force in May 1934.

Westland IV prototype G-EBXX

Desoutter 1 G-AATI was re-registered ZK-ACJ in New Zealand in December 1930

44

Westland Wessex G-ACHI at Yeovil in June 1935

Desoutter DAC 1

The Desoutter DAC 1 was a reworking of Frederick Koolhoven's Cirrus III-powered FK.41, with the tailplane lowered to the thrust line and featuring a remodelled engine cowling.

National Flying Services acquired 19 Desoutters, which it used for flying instruction, joyriding and air-taxi work, but the company ceased operations in 1933 and the surviving aircraft were dispersed. Some 28 Desoutter Mk Is were built and they served all over the world on a variety of tasks. Two were used by the British Red Cross Society as air ambulances, and G-AATI *Aorangi* was flown to New Zealand from Croydon, leaving on February 9, 1930. It arrived in Sydney on March 23 and was shipped the rest of the way.

Wessex G-ACHI, used by Imperial Airways

Cutty Sark G-AAIP with Gipsy II engines

Saro Cutty Sark

This attractive yet workmanlike flying boat was the first product of the fledgling Saunders-Roe company at Cowes, Isle of Wight. The prototype, G-AAIP, was powered by two 105 hp Cirrus Hermes I engines and flew for the first time at Cowes on July 4, 1929. It was later fitted out as an amphibian and operated by S. Kirston and R. Mace on a passenger service between Woolston (Southampton) and St Helier (Jersey). In 1932 this air-craft passed into the hands of Campbell Shaw and Tommy Rose, who put it to work with their newly formed Isle of Man Air Service, and it was finally scrapped in 1935.

In all, twelve Cutty Sarks were built, seven of which were initially registered in Britain. One (S1575) was supplied to the RAF and the remainder were exported. The second aircraft built was VH-UNV for Matthews Aviation in Australia, which took delivery in 1930, and the third Cutty Sark went to the New Zealand Air Force.

Unique among Cutty Sarks was G-ABVF, which was powered by a single 240 hp Armstrong Siddeley Lynx IVC radial engine and fitted with long-range fuel tanks and blind-flying equipment for Japanese pilot Yoshihara's San Francisco-Japan flight. Two others went to the Far East: VR-HAY for the Far East Flying School in Hong Kong, and an unregistered air-craft intended for sale to the Chinese Air Force but which lay unused in Hong Kong until it was returned to Britain in 1937 and allocated the registration G-AETI. This aircraft was allocated to Air Service Training Ltd at Hamble and was scrapped in February 1940. Two other well known Hamble aircraft were G-ACDP and 'CDR, which soldiered on as training aircraft until 1938.

Cutty Sark G-ABBC *Progress*

Blackburn Segrave

Originally conceived by the extraordinary Sir Henry Segrave, this aircraft was derived from the Saro-built Segrave Meteor, which flew for the first time from Cowes, Isle of Wight, on May 28, 1930. The prototype Meteor, G-AAXP, was of mixed wood and metal construction. But when the Blackburn Aeroplane Co took over production after Segrave's accidental death (in the speedboat *Miss England II*) in June 1930, the fuselage was redesigned as a semi-monocoque metal structure. Designated Blackburn-Segrave

Meteor and later simply Blackburn Segrave, two aircraft, G-ABFP and 'BFR, were completed in 1931. A third machine, 'BZJ, remained half completed from the end of 1932 until it emerged a year later as the Blackburn CA 20 Segrave II, complete with a brand-new single-spar, highly tapered wing designed by F. Duncanson. Re-registered G-ACMI, this aircraft flew for the first time early in 1934.

The prototype had a short but full life, competing without honours in the 1930 King's Cup Air

Race and later flying to Italy for demonstrations at the request of the Italian Air Force. Its performance impressed the Italians, who signed a licence agreement to build the type as the Piaggio P.12 trainer. It is believed that of an initial batch of six laid down, only two were built and flown. The prototype, 'AXP, was scrapped at Brough in September 1932.

First of the production Segraves, 'BFP, was first registered to West End store owner Gordon Selfridge in March 1931 before being sold to British Air Naviga-

tion Co at Heston in February 1932 for air-taxi work. Its commercial career was short, however, and after passing back into private hands it was eventually withdrawn from use after its certificate of airworthiness expired in March 1934.

The second Segrave, 'BFR, was first flown at Brough in April 1932 and operated for some months on the Hull-Grimsby ferry service across the Humber. It was finally withdrawn from use after air-taxi and instructional use at Redhill between May 1936 and the end of 1937.

The first production Blackburn Segrave, G-ABFP

The prototype Segrave Meteor, G-AAXP

Avro 618 Ten VH-UMG *Southern Star*

Avro Ten and Five

The Avro 618 Ten was a licence-built version of the tough and successful Fokker F.VIIB/3m. Called the Ten because it carried a crew of two and eight passengers, this three-engined transport was externally similar to the Dutch-built aircraft but differed in minor details.

Avro built fourteen of these aircraft, five of which went to Kingsford-Smith's Australian National Airways. Flagship of that fleet was VH-UMF *Southern Cloud*, first registered in Britain as G-AADM and exhibited in those markings at the 1929 Olympia Aero Show. This aircraft was lost over the Strathbozie Mountains between Sydney and Melbourne on March 21, 1931; the wreck was not discovered until October 1958. Other aircraft of the ANA fleet were VH-UMG *Southern Star*, 'UMH *Southern Sky*, 'UMI *Southern Moon* and 'UNA *Southern Sun*.

Imperial Airways operated two Tens: G-AASP *Achilles*, which it acquired in April 1931, and 'BLU *Apollo*, which was delivered in June of that year. Both aircraft went initially to the Middle East for desert pipeline patrols with the Iraq Petroleum Co and returned to Europe for charter work in June 1933. *Apollo* was destroyed in December 1938 after striking a radio mast in fog; *Achilles* survived until April 1940.

Four aircraft were built for Indian State Airways in 1931, but for one reason or another the order was cut back to one aircraft (VT-ACT), which was used by the Viceroy. Of the remainder, two were sold to the Egyptian Army Air Force and the third was completed for the internal service of Midland and Scottish Air Ferries; registered G-ACGF, it was delivered in May 1933. One Avro Ten did ultimately find its way to Indian National Airways. This was VT-AFX, one of the two Egyptian Air Force aircraft which reached Delhi in September 1934.

A scaled-down version of the Ten, powered by Armstrong Siddeley Genet Majors and called the Avro Five, was shown alongside the Ten at the 1929 Olympia Show. Carrying a pilot and four passengers, this Roy Chadwick design was supplied to Wilson Airways in Nairobi,

Kenya, at the end of the year, registered VP-KAE and named *Knight of the Grail*. A second, VP-KAD *Knight Errant*, was supplied the following February. A third was acquired by the Queensland Air Navigation Co to supplement its two Tens. The final Avro Five to be built was G-AASO, which was operated by Wilson Airways in Kenya from September 1930 until it was damaged beyond repair near Broken Hill in January 1932.

A slightly larger version, with a widened cockpit for two pilots side-by-side and engines attached directly to the underside of the wings, appeared in May 1930. This was the Avro Six, three of which were built. The prototype, G-AAYR, was converted to Avro Five standard with underslung engines and angled windscreen in 1931 and sold to the Far East Aviation Co in Hong Kong, which eventually disposed of it, along with VR-HBF, to the Chinese Government in January 1932. Third of the Avro Sixes was G-ABBY, converted to a six-seat Avro Five in 1933 and supplied to Air Service Training at Hamble.

Avro 619 Five VP-KAE
Knight of the Grail

Close-up of the Genet Major engines installed in Avro Five VP-KAE

H.P.42W G-AAXF *Helena*

The first H.P.42E, G-AAGX *Hannibal*

H.P.42W G-AAXE *Hengist* **at Croydon**

Handley Page H.P.42

The supremely elegant H.P.42 epitomises the best of commercial air travel in the 1930s. Designed for Imperial Airways to succeed the Argosies and Hercules on the airline's Empire airmail route to India, this gracious and economical aircraft served with distinction from November 1931 until after the outbreak of the Second World War.

Two versions were required by Imperial Airways: the European or Western type and the Eastern type; deliveries of the first were to run from December 1930 to March 1931, with the Eastern examples being handed over between September 1930 and January 1931. Handley Page was contracted to build four of each type at unit prices of £23,000 for the European version and £22,000 for the Eastern. Design work began in earnest in January 1929, and by the time of the Olympia Aero Exhibition in July that year the company was

able to show a wooden fuselage mock-up and a scale model of the complete aircraft.

Taxiing tests of the first H.P.42E, G-AAGX, began on October 31, 1930, with the first true flight away from the airfield being made on November 14. It was a success, as were the remainder of the test sorties, and by early June 1931 the prototype, by now named *Hannibal*, was making its first proving flight on the London-Paris route.

Thereafter, H.P.42s were added to the fleet at monthly intervals, the other H.P.42Es being registered G-AAUC *Horsa*, 'AUD *Hanno* and 'AUE *Hadrian*; the H.P.42Ws were registered 'AXC *Heracles*, 'AXD *Horatius*, 'AXE *Hengist* and 'AXF *Helena*. The choice of these wonderfully evocative names was inspired by Imperial Airways' new policy of drawing on history and mythology instead of geography for its aircraft names.

Apart from accidents at the beginning of the careers of both *Hannibal* and *Heracles* which resulted in both aircraft being out of commission for a matter of weeks, the eight aircraft operated largely without incident for practically the whole decade. By September 11, 1938, seven years after its first scheduled flight, *Heracles* had completed 1¼ million miles and carried some 95,000 passengers in Pullman-like comfort. Although utilisation figures for the Eastern and Western versions were comparable, the Western aircraft had higher load figures since they carried up to 38 passengers against the 18-24 of the Eastern model, which had twice the baggage space.

First of the H.P.42s to go was *Hengist*, converted to H.P.42E standard in 1935 and destroyed in a hangar fire at Karachi in May 1937. At the outbreak of war the Croydon-based machines

(which included *Hanno*, converted to H.P.42W standard to replace *Hengist* on European services) were transferred to Whitchurch, from which they were used for ferrying supplies to France. On November 7, 1939, *Horatius* was destroyed at Tiverton, Devon, during a forced landing.

In early 1940 it was decided to recall the H.P.42Es, *Hannibal*, *Horsa*, *Hadrian* and *Helena*. On March 1 *Hannibal* left Delhi with four crew and four passengers; after leaving Jask for Sharjah the aircraft disappeared over the Gulf of Oman and no trace of it was ever found. *Hanno* and *Heracles* were destroyed at Whitchurch in a gale on March 19, 1940, leaving only *Horsa*, *Hadrian* and *Helena* to be posted to No 271 Squadron at Doncaster, where they wore the serials AS981, 982 and 983 respectively. They did not survive beyond the end of the year.

G-AAGX *Hannibal* **under inspection by the AA in July 1931**

Vickers Viastra

Viastra II VH-UOO at Brooklands in 1930

The Vickers Viastra was noteworthy not so much for its unattractiveness as for its durable corrugated-metal structure. Its appearance can best be described as workmanlike, with two 230 hp Armstrong Siddeley Lynx Major engines mounted on the wing struts and a third bolted onto the nose. The fuselage of the prototype, G-AAUB, was built at Crayford but later transferred to the Supermarine works at Woolston for finishing. First flight took place at Hamble on October 1, 1930, with Mutt Summers at the controls.

The ten-passenger aircraft attracted the interest of Norman Brearley, who ordered two Viastra IIs, each powered by a pair of 525 hp geared Bristol Jupiter XIFs, and one Viastra VI powered by a single 540 hp Bristol Jupiter IXF. The two Viastra IIs, registered VH-UOO and 'UOM, were popular with passengers even though they suffered more than their fair share of engine failures. VH-UOM was written

de Havilland D.H.80 Puss Moth

The high-wing, three-seat Puss Moth, designed as a comfortable mount for private pilots, flew for the first time at Stag Lane on September 9, 1929, registered G-AAHZ. Although superficially similar to the D.H.75 Hawk Moth, the smaller Puss Moth was far more successful commercially, achieving almost overnight acceptance. The prototype was later sent to Australia, where it was allocated the registration VH-UON left vacant by the cancellation of the Viastra VI order.

Production at Stag Lane ran to 259 aircraft, almost half of which were exported for light commercial use. So many and varied were the users that it would be impossible to mention more than a few from a list which reads like an international *Who's Who*.

The Puss Moth suffered the sort of accident rate typical of aircraft during those years, trouble eventually being traced to flutter. The trouble was cured by such devices as mass-balanced ailerons and a larger rudder. Nevertheless, the Puss

off in a crash in Western Australia in October 1933, but 'UOO lasted until 1936, when West Australian Airways was incorporated into Australian National Airways. The single-engined Viastra VI, VH-UON, never arrived in Australia but was re-registered G-ABVM and later dismantled at Brooklands.

The prototype Viastra I was fitted with two 490 hp Arm-strong Siddeley Jaguar VIC radials in 1930 and redesignated Viastra III. The following year another engine change, this time to three 450 hp Jupiter VIFMs, led to another change in designation, to Viastra VIII.

The final Viastra was G-ACCC, a Mk X fitted with two 650 hp Bristol Pegasus radials in nacel-les attached directly to the wings. It was to have been used as the official transport of the then Prince of Wales and made its first flight at Hamble in April 1933. Rarely used for its official purpose and modified in 1935 for use as a radio testbed, 'CCC was scrapped in 1937

Prototype Viastra I G-AAUB at Brooklands

Puss Moth G-ABSB of Hillmans Airways

Moth claimed some lives, the most famous casualty being Bert Hinkler, who was killed flying CF-APK across the Alps en route to Australia.

Puss Moth UN-PAX of the Bata Shoe Company

Spartan Three-Seater G-ABTR

Spartan Three-Seater

This conventional little single-bay biplane was one of the better known joyriding aircraft, although relatively few were built. A successor to the 1928 Simmonds Spartan, the Hermes-powered Three-Seater was built at Cowes, Isle of Wight, from 1930 to 1932. In all, 19 Mk Is were built, commencing with Shanklin Flying Services' G-ABAZ *Island Queen*. Only VH-URB was exported, going to Western Australia, where it crashed in October 1938.

By the middle of 1932 the need had arisen for a modified Three-Seater providing both better pilot visibility and easier entry and exit for passengers. This was the Three-Seater Mk II, the prototype of which, G-ABTR, flew for the first time in June 1932. Six production Mk IIs were built.

General Aircraft Monospar series

The Monospar series of twin-engined monoplanes resulted from studies by Swiss-born engineer H. J. Steiger of new methods of making high-strength/weight-ratio cantilever wings. First to be built was an experimental wing designated ST-1, made to Air Ministry order and exhibited at the 1929 Olympia Aero Show. Steiger subsequently formed the Monospar Wing Co with F. F. Crocombe, A. E. L. Chorlton, C. W. Hayward and ex-Martlesham test pilot and sometime air racer Rollo de Haga Haig. The company's first product was the ST-2 wing, again built to Air Ministry order. The team was concurrently building an experimental low-wing cabin monoplane powered by two 50 hp British Salmson AD 9 radial engines. Designated the Monospar ST-3 and carrying the registration G-AARP, it flew for the first time in the summer of 1931.

Encouraged by the ST-3's performance, a new company, General Aircraft Ltd, was formed to develop the Monospar wing patents. Its first product was the ST-4, the prototype of which, G-ABUZ, first flew in May 1932. Orders for five had been received during construction of the prototype and these were delivered during the latter part of 1932 and over the following year. Customers included Portsmouth, Southsea and Isle of Wight Aviation Ltd, the Maharajah of Patiala and several private owners. Production of the improved ST-4 Mk II ran to 22 aircraft, of which 14 were British-registered. The overseas

Spartan passenger accommodation in the Spartan Three-Seater

orders came from customers as far apart as the Jodhpur Flying Club in India (VT-ADW), the Japanese Asahi Newspaper Co (J-BBDA) and the Brazilian airline VASP.

The Pobjoy-powered ST-4 was succeeded by the similarly powered ST-6, much improved by the addition of a manually operated retractable undercarriage. Improvements to the cabin contours provided enough room for an occasional fifth passenger, but only one ST-6, G-ACGI, was operated commercially for any length of time.

The Pobjoy Niagara-powered ST-10 was the first type to be built at General Aircraft's new factory at Hanworth Air Park, to which the company had moved on the closure of the old Croydon works in 1933. Despite winning the 1934 King's Cup Air Race (at an average speed of just over 134 mph) this much improved Monospar never entered series production, prototype G-ACGI eventually going to Portsmouth, Southsea and Isle of Wight Aviation and the other ST-10, VH-UST, being destroyed in a mid-air collision with a de Havilland Gipsy Moth near Sydney in November 1939.

The ST-11 was a Gipsy Major-powered variant for Australia, only two of which were built: VH-UAZ for the Department of Civil Aviation and VH-USN for Eastern Air Transport. These aircraft were fitted with retractable undercarriage, unlike the ten Gipsy Major-powered ST-12s, which had fixed gear. Built during 1935, the majority of the ST-12s went abroad, four to Australia, one to Spain and another to France.

Prototype Monospar ST-3 G-AARP

Prototype Monospar ST-4 G-ABUZ in 1932

Monospar ST-11 VH-UAZ at Croydon in 1934

Monospar ST-12 G-ADBN in 1935

Short Kent

The Short Kent flying boat, a larger, four-engined development of the earlier Calcutta, was ordered by Imperial Airways for its Empire route to Cairo after the closing of the Italian seaports to the airline in October 1929. Regarded as one of the most comfortable transports of its time, the Kent carried sixteen passengers in four rows of seats and was equipped with a galley and washing facilities. The crew were also well cared for, being brought in from the cold and accommodated in a relatively spacious enclosed cockpit. More important than passenger capacity, however, was the size of the freight hold, and the Kent was designed to hold as much mail as possible, maximum capacity being some two tons.

Construction of the prototype began in October 1930 and G-ABFA *Scipio* made its first flight from the Medway on February 24, 1931. Thanks largely to the soundness of its predecessor's design, the Kent behaved perfectly from the first and after routine trials was ferried to the Mediterranean in early May. Second of the three Kents to be built, 'BFB, was launched on March 31 and, carrying the name *Sylvanus*, was ferried out to join *Scipio* later in May. The third Kent was G-ABFC *Satyrus*, which was launched on April 30, flying for the first time on May 2, 1931.

By August 1931 all three flying boats were in service, *Scipio* and *Sylvanus* having been repaired following minor accidents. The three continued to enjoy trouble-free operation for some years, each flying an average of more than 4,000 miles per week. First casualty was *Sylvanus*, deliberately set on fire at her moorings at Brindisi on November 9, 1935. The following year, on August 22, *Scipio* was also lost when she landed heavily at Mirabella, Crete, and sank in deep water. *Satyrus* survived to be scrapped at Hythe in June 1938.

Short Kent G-ABFA *Scipio* **at Rochester**

Short Kent G-ABFB on the Medway in March 1931

Short Valetta

Only one Valetta, G-AAJY, was built, and the type was unusual in that it was flown both as a seaplane and as a landplane. It originated from an Air Ministry requirement for a large three-engined floatplane for direct comparison with the Short Calcutta. Construction began early in 1929 and was completed the following May. Although orthodox in appearance the Valetta was in fact revolutionary in concept and construction and her 40ft floats were the largest ever built. The constant-width cabin could accommodate seventeen passengers in six rows, while the two crew sat side-by-side in an enclosed cockpit.

First flight was made by J. Lankester Parker on May 21, 1930, with trials and demonstrations continuing until February 1931, when the Valetta was returned to Rochester from Felixstowe to be prepared for a survey of the Nile and Great Lakes of Central Africa by Sir Alan Cobham. The survey began on July 22 and the Valetta returning to Rochester at the beginning of September after covering a total of 12,300 miles.

During the winter Short replaced the floats with a wheeled undercarriage and in this form the Valetta was flown for the first time by Lankester Parker in May 1932. After an appearance at the RAF display at Hendon on June 25, 1932, it was flown to Martlesham to seek acceptance as a commercial landplane. It proved unsuitable for this role, however, and was retained as a radio testbed. Martlesham wrote the Valetta off in December 1933 and this interesting experiment ended its days as an instructional airframe at the Radio School at Halton.

Short Valetta in landplane configuration

Short Valetta seaplane G-AAJY makes its maiden flight on May 21, 1930

Prototype Airspeed AS.4 Ferry *Youth of Britain* **of
Alan Cobham's Flying Circus before delivery**

Airspeed AS.4 Ferry

A triumph of utility over aesthetics, the Tiltman-designed AS.4 Ferry was built to the requirements of Airspeed director Sir Alan Cobham, who wanted a small multi-engined airliner for his National Aviation Day tours. Cobham placed an order for two ten-passenger Ferries in June 1931 at a price of £5,195 each, and the prototype, G-ABSI, was rolled out at the end of March 1932. After some adventures while moving the airframe from the factory at York to the Yorkshire Aero Club at Sherburn-in-Elmet, the first flight was made on April 5.

Named *Youth of Britain II*, the prototype Ferry was delivered to Cobham on April 24, almost a fortnight after the inauguration of National Aviation Day. It was joined in early June by the second Ferry, 'BSJ, naturally named *Youth of Britain III*, and the two silver-and-green aircraft rapidly built up a solid reputation for hard work and high serviceability, logging some 640 hours between them in the first season, making more than 9,000 landings and carrying 92,000 passengers. In 1934 'BSJ was sold to the Himalaya Air Transport and Survey Co and re-registered VT-AFO. Christened *Dragoman*, it served for almost two years, transporting pilgrims to the shrine at Badrinath before being destroyed on the ground by vandals at Delhi in October 19, 1936.

A second pair of Ferries, 'CBT and 'CFB, were bought by Midland and Scottish Air Ferries, the first being delivered from York in February 1933 and the second, from Airspeed's new Portsmouth factory, in June. During the summers of 1933 and 1934 the two aircraft flew from Renfrew to Campbeltown, Belfast and Speke. But then increasing competition forced MSAF managing director John Sword to close down and put the aircraft up for sale.

G-ABPI flying as *Atalanta* in 1932

G-ABTI, the true Imperial Airways *Atalanta*

Armstrong Whitworth A.W.15 Atalanta

Armstrong Whitworth's sleek Atalanta was a fair example of art deco, the design fashion of the time. Armstrong Whitworth designer John Lloyd approached Imperial Airways' brief for a nine-passenger, four-engined mail-carrying aircraft with characteristic originality, breaking away from the accepted biplane layout to produce a relatively small monoplane powered by four 340 hp Armstrong Siddeley Double Mongoose engines faired into the wing leading edge. Eschewing a retractable undercarriage, which was still looked upon with a certain amount of suspicion at that time, Lloyd provided the Atalanta with a novel spatted arrangement in which the oleo legs and divided axle were housed entirely within the fuselage. In service, however, the spats were replaced by simple stone-guards to facilitate servicing.

First flight of the prototype, G-ABPI Atalanta, was made on June 6, 1932, and by September two more, registered 'BTG and 'BTH, had been completed. The remaining five aircraft of the Imperial Airways contract were completed by the following April. Atalanta flew the airline's first A.W.15 service from Croydon to Brussels and Cologne on September 26, 1932, and, together with 'BTG Amalthea and 'BTH Andromeda, was used on the London-Brussels and London-Paris-Basle-Zurich routes until the beginning of 1933.

In late October 1932 Atalanta was badly damaged in a forced landing and the name was transferred to the fourth A.W.15, 'BTI, the rebuilt 'BPI later receiving the name Arethusa. In early January 1933 the newly named Atalanta left Croydon on a long proving flight to Cape Town and remained in South Africa following its arrival on February 14, to be joined later by Amalthea, Andromeda and 'BTJ Artemis.

Imperial Airways also had plans to use the A.W.15s on another Empire route, the extension of the London-Karachi service all the way to Singapore, where it was intended to link up with Qantas D.H.86s. Subsequently this service was operated by an Imperial Airways' subsidiary company, Indian Trans-Continental Airways, and Arethusa and 'BTM Aurora were re-registered in Indian markings.

Three Atalantas were lost in accidents: 'BTK Athena was burned out in a hangar fire at Delhi in September 1936, Amalthea crashed at Kisumu, Kenya, in July 1938, and Andromeda was dismantled in Egypt after damage to a wing in June 1939. The surviving five aircraft were all impressed for service with the Indian Air Force in March 1941, and all had been either destroyed or withdrawn from use before the end of the war.

Indian Trans-Continental Airways VT-AEG *Aurora*, ex-G-ABTM

Blackburn Biplane/Monoplane

In much the same way that the Air Ministry had asked Short to produce landplane and seaplane versions of the Valetta for comparison, so Blackburn was asked for a pair of comparative aircraft, the difference being that this time they were to be biplane and monoplane variants. The two aircraft were to be identical in every respect except for wing arrangement, having similar payload and range and the same engines. They were both to carry ten passengers and two crew members.

Construction began at Brough in early 1931 and the first to be completed was the Biplane, G-ABKW, which flew for the first time on June 10, 1932. The Monoplane, 'BKV, was completed four months after the Biplane and flew for the first time on October 4, 1932. Comparative trials were carried out at Martlesham Heath after the 1933 Hendon Air Display in June. At the same all-up weight the Biplane was found to be slower, but the structural weight of the Monoplane was greater so that its payload was correspondingly less.

Neither aircraft was ever used commercially by the intended owner, Imperial Airways, because a fleet of much larger Short Calcuttas and D.H.66 Hercules was already operating on the North African route. The Biplane was subsequently scrapped after its registration had been cancelled in January 1934. The Monoplane was taken over by the RAF, which used it for various instrument and wireless trials. A short period at Cardington ended with its reduction to scrap in December 1937.

Blackburn Biplane G-ABKW and Monoplane G-ABKV

Biplane G-ABKW and . . .

... Monoplane G-ABKV

D.H.83 Fox Moth G-ABVI of Hillmans Airways

Spartan Cruiser

This smart three-engined monoplane was designed by E. W. Percival and built at Cowes in 1931 in collaboration with Saunders-Roe. Derived from the Saro-Percival Mailplane, the Cruiser flew for the first time in May 1932, powered by three 120 hp de Havilland Gipsy III in-line engines. The all-metal fuselage accommodated two crew and up to six passengers. Prototype

G-ABTY was lost in the Channel in May 1935 while in the service of the Hon Mrs Victor Bruce's Channel Air Lines.

Some twelve Cruiser IIs were built, beginning with G-ACBM, which flew for the first time in February 1933. This aircraft had been built for Iraq Airwork Ltd for use on an experimental route between Baghdad and Mosul and after test flying was ferried

out to Iraq carrying the registration YI-AAA. Five Cruiser IIs were sold abroad, with two delivered to the Yugoslav airline Aeroput and two to the Bata shoe company in Czechoslovakia.

In Britain Cruiser IIs were operated by Spartan Air Lines, amongst others, which served an internal route between Heston and Cowes, and United Air-

ways Ltd operating between Heston, Stanley Park, Blackpool and Ronaldsway.

The Cruiser III was slightly larger than its predecessor and could carry up to eight passengers. First flight of this Gipsy Major-engined aircraft was in April 1935. The three Mk IIIs built all went to Spartan Air Lines, later to be absorbed into British Airways in 1936.

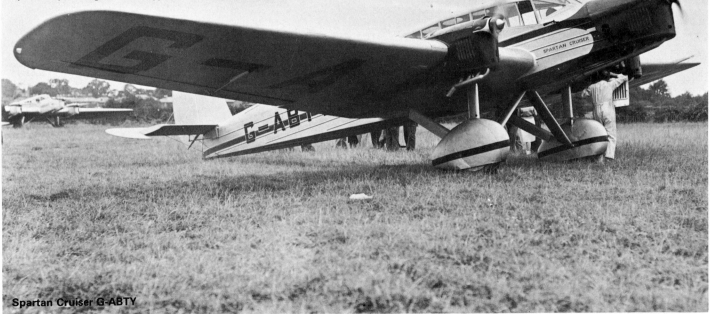

Spartan Cruiser G-ABTY

de Havilland D.H.83 Fox Moth

The attractive four-passenger Fox Moth was designed by A. E. Hagg to take advantage of the increasing worldwide demand for cheap and simple passenger or light freight transports. The D.H.83 had wings, tail, undercarriage and engine mountings in common with the Tiger Moth, while the spruce and plywood fuselage was a return to the earlier de Havilland arrangement of an enclosed cabin forward and an open cockpit halfway along the fuselage.

First flight of the prototype, G-ABUO, took place at Stag Lane on January 29, 1932. This aircraft was later shipped to Canada, where it was evaluated on both floats and skis by Canadian Airways Ltd and, re-registered CF-API, flew usefully until 1950. A total of 98 Fox Moths were built, 49 of which were British-registered. Hillmans

Airways used three on its Clacton-Maylands-Ramsgate service from June 1932, and others were operated by the Scottish carriers Scottish Motor Traction Co and Scottish Air Ferries Ltd, both of Renfrew, which had twelve between them. Fox Moth ferry services were operated between Southend and Rochester, and Portsmouth and Ryde, Isle of Wight.

Fox Moths were to be seen in many parts of the globe throughout their long service life, one even finding its way to Antarctica with the British Graham Land Expedition. In India Tata Airlines used the type on its Bombay-Karachi route, while Indian National Airways operated two between Karachi and Lahore. Others flew commercially in several parts of Africa, and in Australia Qantas replaced its Flying Doctor Service D.H.50s with D.H.83 Fox Moths.

Prototype D.H.83 Fox Moth G-ABUO at Stag Lane

de Havilland D.H.84 Dragon

Yet another design by A. E. Hagg, the twin-engined Dragon was produced to meet a Hillman Airways requirement for an aircraft suitable for its Paris service. Carrying six passengers and a single pilot, the Dragon proved to be outstandingly economical. The prototype, G-ACAN, first flew at Stag Lane on November 24, 1932, and was delivered to Hillman's airfield at Mayfield in December of that year. Hillman had originally ordered four Dragons but the volume of traffic attracted by the airline's low fares prompted an order for an additional two. The complete fleet was then modified to carry eight passengers by the removal of the rear luggage compartments.

This nicely proportioned little aeroplane quickly became popular, and de Havilland ultimately built no fewer than 115 over the next three years. In addition, 87 were built by de Havilland Pty Ltd in Sydney, Australia.

In 1933 de Havilland produced an improved version known as the Dragon 2, externally identifiable by its individually framed windows and faired-in undercarriage struts. Of the 70 Dragons used by British internal airlines, some 31 were Mk 2s, six of which went to Jersey Airlines. Railway Air Services used a similar fleet for its Liverpool-Birmingham-Cardiff-Plymouth and Birmingham-Bristol-Isle of Wight routes.

D.H.84 Dragon G-ACNJ *Rogel Bay* **of Jersey Airways Ltd**

Airspeed AS.5 Courier

Tiltman's single-engined Courier was the first British retractable-undercarriage type to go into quantity production. The story goes that the decision to adopt a low-cantilever-wing configuration was prompted by a photograph of Lockheed's Orion seen in an aviation magazine. Whatever the truth of that story, Airspeed's aim was to build a vehicle suitable for Sir Alan Cobham's proposed non-stop air-refuelling flight to India.

Construction of the prototype began in September 1932 and the completed aircraft, registered G-ABXN, flew for the first time from Portsmouth Airport on April 10, 1933, with former Schneider Trophy pilot G. H. Stainforth at the controls. Cobham's record attempt was abandoned after a wheels-up landing at Hal Far, Malta, but the team had by then succeeded in laying down the basics of in-flight refuelling.

Series production of the Courier began with G-ACJL, delivered to distributor Aircraft Exchange and Mart on September 4, 1933. At this time the manufacturer was offering two basic versions of the Courier: the AS.5A or "English" variant fitted with one 240 hp Armstrong Siddeley Lynx IVC, and the AS.5B "Colonial" variant with the 277 hp Armstrong Siddeley Cheetah V.

Despite being among the most advanced aircraft of its time the Courier did not have a spectacularly successful commercial career, though this was more the result of poor management on the part of the operators than any shortcoming of the aircraft's. London, Scottish and Provincial Airways, for instance, ordered four during 1934 but used only two, G-ACSY and 'SZ, on its internal services. North Eastern Airways was rather more successful and operated prototype ABXN plus ACLF, 'LT and 'VF from Edinburgh to Woolington, Doncaster and Croydon. The other significant operator was Portsmouth, Southsea and Isle of Wight Aviation, which eventually took possession of the survivors, re-engining them with Lynx IVCs and converting them to fixed undercarriage for the Ryde ferry service. All of these aircraft were impressed as air taxis at the outbreak of war, later serving with the Air Transport Auxiliary.

G-ACVF alone survived the war, only to be scrapped after just one season of joyriding with East Anglian Flying Services.

Line-up of four Couriers of Portsmouth, Southsea and IOW Aviation at Portsmouth Airport. Also shown at right are Monospar ST-25 Jubilee G-ADPK, Monospar ST-10 G-ACTS and a Fox Moth

AS.5 Courier G-ACJL of Aircraft Exchange & Mart Ltd

Experimental Rapier-engined Courier G-ACNZ

69

Short Scion

Like most Short aircraft, the sawn-off S.16 Scion was more functional than attractive. The Scion, moreover, was expected to carry a pilot and five passengers on the power of its two 75 hp Pobjoy R radials. Registered G-ACJI, the prototype flew for the first time from Gravesend Airport on August 18, 1933, with J. Lankester Parker at the controls.

The first production batch of Scion 1s, registered G-ACUV to 'UZ, was powered by 90 hp Pobjoy Niagara IIIs; the first of these aircraft was assembled in time to appear at the Hendon SBAC Show in July 1934. Parker and Harold Piper flew 'JI and 'UW on a series of more than 1,000 ferry flights between Rochester and Southend, quickly establishing a reputation for excellent reliability. This series of flights led to the introduction of an improved version designated Scion 2, on which the engine thrust line was raised and a sixth passenger seat was added. This series began with 'CUZ (originally to have been Scion 1) and embraced ten Short-built aircraft, plus a further six built by Pobjoy. British operators included Southend Flying Services, which together with Short, operated the Rochester-Southend ferry with Scion 2 'DDN and Scion 1 'CUY respectively during 1935 and 1936. Scottish operators were West of Scotland Airways with Scion 2 'DDP and Aberdeen Airways with Scion 1 'CUV.

Overseas, Scions found their way to aviation-hungry Australia, which eventually absorbed one Mk 1 (VH-UUP, ex-G-ACUX) and four Mk 2s. The outbreak of war saw eleven Scions of both versions impressed for use by the RAF on a variety of tasks. Of these only 'EZF re-emerged in civilian colours after the war, lasting until 1954. The Australian aircraft lasted rather better, with two still airworthy as late as 1966.

Short Scion 2 G-ACUZ

Scion 1 G-ACUX on floats

Boulton and Paul P.64 Mailplane and P.71A

The Boulton and Paul P.64 was designed by J. D. North to Air Ministry Specification 21/28, which called for an aircraft with a crew of two and capable of carrying up to 175 cu ft of mail. Powered by two 555 hp Bristol Pegasus IM.2 radial engines, the prototype and only example built, G-ABYK, was first flown at Mousehold, Norwich, in March 1933 by Sqn Ldr C. A. Rea. Sadly, the aircraft was wrecked following an unexplained dive during the third test flight of the Martelsham trials on October 21, 1933, and the pilot, Flt Lt G. L. G. Richmond, was killed.

The P.71A was a lightened version of the P.64 with a longer and slimmer fuselage and new triple-fin tail. Two aircraft were built: G-ACOX *Boadicea* and 'COY *Britomart*, both powered by two 490 hp Armstrong Siddeley Jaguar VIA radial engines. Both aircraft were delivered to Imperial Airways at Croydon in February 1935 and there fitted out as seven-seat VIP transports or light freighters. Both aircraft were subsequently lost, *Boadicea* in a landing accident at Haren, Brussels, in October 1935 and *Britomart* in the English Channel in September 1936.

Boulton and Paul P.64 Mailplane

Boulton and Paul P.71A G-ACOY *Britomart*

Prototype BA Eagle G-ACRG

Vickers Vellox

The only Vellox built, G-ABKY, was originally laid down by Vickers as a twin-engined Vellore, with the wings and tail of the original aircraft mated to a new fuselage of larger cross-section. Fitted out for ten passengers, a steward and a flight crew of two, it flew for the first time at Brooklands on January 23, 1934. After flight trials at Martlesham Heath the Pegasus-engined Vellox was sold in May 1936 to Imperial Airways, which used it for night freighting. The Vellox was not particularly successful in this role and was finally burned out in August 1936 following a night take-off crash at Croydon Airport.

BA Eagle

This fast three-seat monoplane was designed by George Handasyde for British Klemm Aeroplane Co and the prototype, G-ACRG, flew for the first time at Hanworth in early 1934. Powered by a 130 hp de Havilland Gipsy Major engine and featuring a manually retractable undercarriage, the Eagle attracted the attention of racing and record-attempt pilots, but to begin with was not overwhelmingly successful as a competition aircraft.

Only six Eagle Mk Is were built: four were registered in Britain, one of which was later exported; CR-MAI went to Portuguese East Africa; and VH-USP was acquired by Adastra Airways of Sydney, Australia.

An improved de luxe model, the Eagle 2, began to appear at the very end of 1934, the first aircraft, G-ACZT, being registered on December 18. Some 37 Eagle 2s were built, 22 of which were registered in Britain. Main external differences from the Mk 1 were a new rudder, a deepened rear fuselage and revised door.

Prototype BA Eagle G-ACRG

The only Type 212 Vickers Vellox, G-ABKY

The only Avro 642/2m, G-ACFV

Avro 642

A derivative of the Avro Five and Ten series, the 642 was built in both twin and four-engined versions. First to be completed was the 642/2m, powered by a pair of 460 hp Armstrong Siddeley Jaguar VID radials mounted on an Avro Ten wing lowered to the shoulder position. Fitted out for 16 passengers and two crew, the prototype, G-ACFV, was delivered to Midland and Scottish Air Ferries at Renfrew in April 1934. Sold to Commercial Air Hire of Croydon in May 1935 after MSAF ceased operations, 'CFV was used extensively for early-morning Continental newspaper delivery flights for two seasons before changing its identity to VH-UXD in September 1936 after W. R. Carpenter & Co bought it for mail services in New Guinea. It was destroyed by the Japanese in 1942.

The second 642 was a four-engined variant powered by 240 hp Lynx IVCs and named *Star of India*. This neat-looking seven-seater was built for the Viceroy of India, Lord Willington, to replace Avro Ten VT-ACT. Registered VY-AFM, the 642/4m remained in service at Delhi for several years and was finally withdrawn in 1940.

Airspeed AS.6 Envoy

The Envoy was a twin-engined development of the Courier, designed to carry six to eight passengers and embodying the same sort of structure as its single-engined predecessor. The prototype, G-ACMT, flew for the first time on June 26, 1934, powered by a pair of 185 hp Wolseley AR 9 radials. Altogether Airspeed built 16 Envoy Mk Is (including the prototype) powered by a bewildering variety of engines, ranging from the AR 9s of 'CMT to Armstrong Siddeley Lynx IVCs or Cheetahs.

First significant commercial user of Envoys was North Eastern Airways, which acquired G-ADAZ *Tynedale*, 'DBB *Wharfedale* and 'DBZ *Swaledale* during March and April 1935 for its Edinburgh-Heston service. Sadly, lack of passengers contributed to the early closure of this run in July, although it was resurrected in the summer of 1936 over a slightly different route.

Commercial operators abroad were comparatively plentiful, and Envoys were flown by the Japanese Air Transportation Co on a Japan-Manchuria service from the summer of 1935. These aircraft were joined by others built under licence in Japan by Mitsubishi at Nagoya.

In 1936 Airspeed modified the prototype to Mk II standard by fitting flaps and more powerful Lynx engines. This aircraft was destroyed during the Spanish Civil War. Production aircraft totalled seven machines, all destined for South Africa for use by either the air force or South Africa Airways.

Of the 26 Mk IIIs built, four were AS.6Es for the Czechoslovakian state airline's Prague-Moscow route, opened in August 1935. AS.6K operators included French carrier Air Pyrenees, which ordered six Czechoslovakian operator Victorise Mill and Steel Co of Prague, and the Maharajahs of Jaipur and Indore. British AS.6J users included the King's Flight, which had the immaculately turned-out G-AEXX, and the two Brooklands instructors Max Findlay and Ken Waller, whose G-AENA, specially prepared for the Schlesinger Race from Portsmouth to Johannesburg, crashed on take-off from Abercorn, Northern Rhodesia, on October 1, 1936, killing Findlay.

Envoy III OK-BAL for Czechoslovakia

Envoy I G-ACMT

Interior of Envoy II

de Havilland D.H.86

The ten-passenger, four-engined D.H.86 was designed and built to an Australian specification for a mail and passenger aircraft capable of operating safely across the Java and Timor seas on the Singapore-Australia sector of the proposed Empire Air Route extension. The prototype, G-ACPL, was flown for the first time at Stag Lane by Hubert Broad on January 14, 1934. The aircraft was originally designed for single-pilot operation with a wireless operator/navigator sitting behind and slightly to the right of him, but the Qantas/Imperial Airways order stipulated two-pilot operation and the prototype was subsequently fitted with an elongated two-seat nose which added to the attractiveness of this well-proportioned aircraft.

First commercial flights were undertaken by the three single-pilot D.H.86s of Railway Air Services, starting in late May 1934. In addition to 'CPL, RAS used 'CVY *Mercury* and 'CVZ *Jupiter* on its Croydon-Castle Bromwich-Barton-Belfast-Renfrew services.

Overseas the type did not have a particularly auspicious start to its career. The first production machine, VH-URN, disappeared off Wilson's Promonotory on October 19, 1934, with the loss of the owner, Victor Holyman of Holyman's Airways. This tragedy was closely followed by the loss of one of the six Qantas aircraft near Longreach on November 15. Holyman Airways lost a second D.H.86 off Flinders Island in the following October; the airline was taken over by Australian National Airways in July 1936.

In Britain Jersey Airways acquired six D.H.86s to replace its Dragons on the Heston-Eastleigh-Channel Islands run, while Hillman Airways used three on its Stapleford-Paris route. During the latter part of 1935 de Havilland introduced an improved version, the D.H.86A, with pneumatic undercarriage legs, larger wheel brakes and tailwheel, new rudder and steeper windshield. The following year saw the introduction of 12 of the improved aircraft by Imperial Airways on its European network and on the Khartoum-Accra sector of the Empire route, which was inaugurated during February 1936. In March the airline inaugurated the Penang-Saigon-Hong Kong shuttle with 'CWD *Dorado*.

The D.H.86B, introduced in the early part of 1937, was a standard aircraft modified by the addition of large auxiliary fins to the tailplane tips; all D.H.86As were retrospectively modified to this standard. Ten production D.H.86Bs were built: three went to Australia, four to Turkey, and the other three remained in Britain.

During the Second World War D.H.86s were used all over the world on a variety of tasks, ranging from air ambulance work in the Western Desert to freighting in France. Many survived the war, including the original Qantas aircraft, VH-USC *Canberra*, and several British aircraft, among them G-ACVY, 'CZP, 'DYH and 'ENR, which reverted to Railway Air Services in 1946 until withdrawn in 1948. Last of this type was the ex-Jersey Airways G-ACZP, which was damaged beyond repair at Madrid in September 1958.

D.H.86 VH-UUA *Adelaide*, ex-Imperial Airways G-ACWE

D.H.86 G-ACVZ of Railway Air Services in December 1934

D.H.89A Dragon Rapide G-AFEZ of British European Airways

BEA Dragon Rapide at Southampton

de Havilland D.H.89 Dragon Rapide

Another of those aircraft which almost everybody seems to have heard of, the Dragon Rapide was a scaled-down version of the D.H.86 powered by two 200 hp de Havilland Gipsy Six engines. The prototype, which flew for the first time at Hatfield on April 17, 1934, was first of no fewer than 728 Rapides.

First commercial operator was Hillman Airways, closely followed by Railway Air Services, which operated eight Rapides on its Croydon-Speke-Renfrew-Belfast routes. Abroad, Rapides were supplied to KLM, Canadian Airways, the state airlines of Turkey, Persia, Romania and Jugoslavia, and countless small operators in every continent.

In 1937 production Rapides were fitted with small flaps on the lower wings, resulting in a designation change to D.H.89A. Shortly after the outbreak of the Second World War the majority of Rapides in Britain were impressed into the Air Transport Auxiliary, while others at home and abroad were used by the armed forces of Britain and the Commonwealth. Aircraft built during the war were designated D.H.89B Dominie and used in Mk 1 form as navigation and radio trainers and in Mk 2 form as communications aircraft. After the war large numbers of these economical and robust aircraft were put up for sale and many were returned to civil use. One of the largest post-war operators was British European Airways, which used the type on its Scottish, Scilly and Channel Islands routes.

Dominie civil conversion G-ALAT

D.H.89 Dominie G-AHKB

G-ACJJ *Scylla*

Short L.17 G-ACJJ *Scylla* **in 1934**

Short L.17 Scylla

The Short L.17 landplane was not a brand-new design but a modification of the S.17 Kent flying boat already in service with Imperial Airways. Registered G-ACJJ and 'CJK and named *Scylla* and *Syrinx* respectively, the two L.17s built had the same wings and tail unit as the Kent. The new fuselage was a simple semi-monocoque with unstressed aluminium skin on braced floor and side frames.

First to fly was *Scylla*, on March 26, 1934, with J. Lankester Parker at the controls. By the time *Scylla* had completed its Martlesham trials and was engaged in crew training at Croydon, the second aircraft had been completed at Rochester and was first flown by Parker on May 17. By mid-June both were in service with Imperial Airways' European service on the Croydon-Paris run. Accommodating up to 38 passengers in their wide and spacious cabins, the L.17s were among the most luxurious aircraft of their time.

Both aircraft were to suffer mishaps during their careers. *Scylla* was damaged in August 1934 when it tipped onto its nose after a brake locked. More serious was the damage done to *Syrinx* during a gale at Brussels in the following November, which necessitated the aircraft's return to Rochester for repairs. At this point the opportunity was taken to replace the trial engines with four 660 hp Bristol Pegasus XCs and to retrim the interior in the colours and materials that were to be used on the Empire flying boats.

At the outbreak of war in September 1939 both machines, along with the other large Imperial Airways aircraft, were moved from Croydon to Whitchurch and used for transporting stores and personnel to France. Requisitioned from National Air Carriers by the RAF in March 1940, neither aircraft survived beyond the end of the year.

G-ACJK *Syrinx* **under inspection by African chiefs at Croydon in July 1934**

Avro 652 Anson

Only two commercial examples of the twin-engined retractable-undercarriage Avro 652 were built, although production of military Ansons was to run to many thousands over the years. Designed by Roy Chadwick, the Anson was a brilliant piece of improvisation in which a fuselage assembly basically similar to that of the earlier Avro-Fokkers was mated to a simple one-piece wooden wing, moved from the high to the low position. Power was provided by a pair of 290 hp Armstrong Siddeley Cheetah VIs in long nacelles which also housed the undercarriage.

First flight of the prototype,

G-ACRM *Avalon*, was made on January 7, 1935, and this and the second aircraft, 'CRN *Avatar* (soon changed to *Ava*), were delivered to Imperial Airways at Croydon in March of that year. The two aircraft saw extensive service on the airline's Croydon-Brindisi route until they were sold to Air Service Training at Hamble in July 1938 for use as navigational trainers. They were impressed into the RAF in February 1941 and handed over to the Royal Navy in July of that year.

After the end of the war a large number of surplus Anson 1s, distinguished from the Avro 652 by their large windows and

more powerful Cheetah IX engines, were adapted for commercial use, proving particularly suitable for the numerous small charter companies which sprang up at that time. Some 98 of these aircraft were registered in the UK alone, while no fewer than 140 were registered in Australia. Although simple and quite reliable, the Anson 1s could not be expected to last for ever, and in 1960 deterioration of the glue joints in the wooden wings meant that no more certificates of airworthiness could be granted. The last British-registered Anson 1 finished its career in 1962, while in Australia the axe finally fell on the last machine in June 1962.

Avro 652 G-ACRM

D.H.90 Dragonfly VP-YAX of Rhodesia and Nyasaland Airways Ltd before delivery

G-ACRM

IMPERIAL AIRWAYS LONDON

de Havilland D.H.90 Dragonfly

The little five-seat D.H.90 Dragonfly was more than just a scaled-down Rapide, incorporating as it did structural details first seen on the 1934 D.H.88 Comet racers. Immediately noticeable was the simplicity of the inter-wing bracing, achieved through the use of a more than usually robust centre section. Powered by a pair of 130 hp de Havilland Gipsy Major engines, the prototype, G-ADNA, flew for the first time at Hatfield on August 12, 1935.

A total of 66 production Dragonflies was built, 21 of which were initially registered in Britain. Several of these went to private owners such as Sir Philip Sassoon, Lord Beaverbrook and Sir W. Lindsay Everard. But the type was more suited to commercial operation, particularly abroad, where the Dragonfly was entirely at home in the extremely varied climatic conditions of Australia and East Africa.

With the outbreak of the Second World War some 14 British-registered Dragonflies were impressed for communications duties within the aero industry, but shortage of spares and the difficulty of repairing the monocoque fuselage allowed only a handful to survive the war.

Heston Phoenix

The five-seat, high-wing Heston Type 1 Phoenix was conventional in most respects, being of orthodox wooden construction, but had the distinction of a hydraulically operated retractable undercarriage housed in the ample fairings of the N-type wing bracing struts. Designed by George Cornwall, the prototype Phoenix, G-ADAD, flew for the first time on August 18, 1935.

Only six were built, of which one was for export. This was the Australian-registered VH-AJM, built for C. J. Melrose's "Adelaide to Anywhere" air-taxi service. Sadly, this aircraft was destroyed with the loss of both occupants when it crashed near Melbourne on July 5, 1936, only four months after its arrival in Australia.

In September 1936 'DAD was sold to the Greek air-taxi operator E. Xidis and re-registered SX-AAH. In Britain the type was not a commercial success despite its performance, and the destruction of 'EHJ in September 1939 left only three to be impressed for RAF communications use. One Phoenix did manage to survive the war; this was the ex-Standard Telephones and Cables flying laboratory, Phoenix Mk II G-AESV, which was itself destroyed in a crash in the French Alps during April 1952.

The functional cockpit of Phoenix G-ADAD

Heston Phoenix G-ADAD

General Aircraft Monospar ST-25

The first ST-25 built, G-ADIV, looked much the same as the basic ST-10 but was fitted with accommodation for an occasional fifth passenger. The "25" in the aircraft's designation recognised King George V's Silver Jubilee, an occasion which prompted General Aircraft to bestow the name Jubilee on the type.

Powered by two 90 hp Pobjoy Niagaras, the Jubilee had remarkably good performance despite its somewhat angular shape. 1936 saw the announcement of an improved version, designated the ST-25 De Luxe and powered by the slightly more powerful Niagara III engines. Only one example, G-AEDY, was built. This aircraft, together with ST-10 'CTS, was later to be used in tests of a new twin-rudder tail unit in an attempt to improve directional stability with one engine stopped.

Production of these twin-finned aircraft, designated ST-25 Universal, totalled 26, with five going to East Canada Air Lines in New Brunswick and others finding their way to Romania, Denmark and Turkey.

Monospar ST-25 G-AEDY

Miles Falcon

The Falcon series began with the construction of the prototype M.3, G-ACTM, in 1934 for H. L. Brook to fly in the 1934 MacRobertson England-Australia race. The first production aircraft was M.3A G-ADBF, which first flew at Woodley in January 1935. A total of fifteen M.3As were registered in Britain, with a further three for export.

First flight of a new Gipsy Six-powered variant took place in July 1935. Designated M.3B to M.3F, some 18 Falcon Sixes were built before production ended in 1936. Operators tended to be small air-taxi companies and companies using the type for corporate transport.

The M.4 Merlin was a larger, five-seat, version of the Falcon built in 1935 for Birkett Air Services at Heston, and Tata Air Lines of Bombay. Miles built only four examples of the Merlin, which first flew at Woodley in May 1935.

Miles M.3A Falcon G-ADBF

Short Scion Senior

The four-engined Short Scion Senior was conceived as a higher-capacity successor to the Scion of 1933. Its designers reasoned that the ten-seat Senior could do with one pilot the work of two Scions and two pilots, provided of course that there was enough traffic. The expected orders from ferry operators failed to materialise, however, mostly because these airlines had equipped themselves with the more cost-effective de Havilland Dragon and Dragon Rapide. Nevertheless, an order for three Seniors was forthcoming from the Irrawaddy Flotilla Company in Burma.

The first aircraft, registered G-ACZG, flew for the first time

on October 22, 1935, with J. Lankester Parker at the controls. Later registered VT-AGU, it was shipped to Rangoon in December 1935, being joined by the second Irrawaddy aircraft, VT-AHI, during the following August. The third of the Burmese order, VT-AIJ, was shipped out to Rangoon during December 1936. Short, meanwhile, had built a landplane demonstrator, G-AECU, which flew for the first time on June 15, 1936. After serving for some time as a company hack it was leased to Jersey Airways for the 1938 summer season before being sold to the Iraq Petroleum Transport Co at Haifa in December of that year.

The first of the two British-

operated seaplanes was G-AENX, first flown by Parker on June 22, 1937, and operating initially on the Greenock Harbour-Stornoway service of West of Scotland Air Services. In February 1938 this aircraft was sold to Elders Colonial Airways Ltd in Sierra Leone, which operated 'ENX between Freetown and Bathurst until it was sunk at its moorings in August 1939. Last of the Seniors was G-AETH, originally destined for a ferry service between Sydney Harbour and Newcastle, New South Wales, but actually bought by the Air Ministry and equipped with an experimental half-scale model of the planning hull designed for fitment to the Short Sunderland military flying boat.

**Scion Senior floatplane VT-AGU
of Irrawaddy Flotilla Co**

Short S.23 Empire Flying Boat G-ADVB *Corsair*

Maiden flight of S.23 G-ADUX *Cassiopeia* **in January 1937**

Short Empire Flying Boat

The Short Empire Flying Boats are justifiably among the best remembered commercial aircraft from any nation to come out of the aeronautically fertile 1930s. No fewer than 31 S.23s, nine S.30s and two S.33s were built between 1936 and 1940. Of all-metal flush-riveted construction, the Empire boats were ahead of their time. So impressed was Imperial Airways by the design that the carrier took the unprecedented step of ordering 28 virtually straight off the drawing board. Accommodation was arranged for 24 day passengers or 16 sleeping berths, plus 1½ tons of freight, while the spacious flight deck was laid out for pilot and first officer, seated side-by-side, and a navigator/radio operator. A flight engineer was carried on long flights only.

First flight of the prototype, G-ADHL *Canopus*, took place at Rochester on July 4, 1936, with the second aircraft, 'DHM *Caledonia*, following on July 11. *Canopus* was handed over to Imperial Airways on October 20 and shortly afterwards ferried out to Genoa; the remainder of the fleet followed at a rate of about two per month. Regular services on the Empire routes began at Hythe in the following February, and by the end of the year Imperial Airways had taken delivery of 22 Empire boats, with two more, VH-ABA and 'ABB, ready for collection by Qantas. During 1937, however, Imperial Airways had lost three of its fleet: G-ADVA *Capricornus* crashed on March 24 near Lyons, 'DVC *Courtier* was lost as a result of pilot error when Capt Poole misjudged his height on finals at Phaleron Bay on October 1, and the crew of 'DUZ *Cygnus* attempted with fatal consequences to take off with full flap on December 5 at Brindisi.

In the autumn of 1938 Short introduced the S.30 Empire boats, with Bristol Perseus sleeve-valve engines and higher all-up weight. A total of nine were built, all for Imperial Airways, though three were delivered to Tasman Empire Airways and named *Awarua*, *Aotearoa* and *Australia*. The last-named aircraft was eventually returned to Britain and Imperial Airways, which renamed it *Clare*. Imperial Airways S.30s were used principally on the transatlantic route.

Flight deck of G-ADUT *Centaurus* in April 1938. Pilot is Capt Sheppard

de Havilland D.H.91 Albatross

The sleek and beautiful Albatross was a descendant of the twin-engined D.H.88 Comet built for the 1934 MacRobertson Trophy flights between England Australia. de Havilland had not been slow to realise the potential of a fast, moderately capacious airliner in an age of increasing air-mindedness, but the British Government characteristically failed to grasp the point until the European skies began to fill with Douglas DC-2s. A specification was eventually written for an aircraft capable of carrying 1,000lb of mail 2,500 miles at high speed. A contract was signed with de Havilland in January 1936 and design of the new aircraft was entrusted to the capable A. E. Hagg.

The engine chosen was a brand-new design by Major Frank Halford, who took two Gipsy Six blocks and fitted them to a new crankcase to produce an inverted V-12 rated at 525 hp. The exceptionally clean cowling arrangement for these engines was typical of the approach to the whole airframe, which was claimed to be aerodynamically more than 80% efficient. Construction was all-wood, with the

monocoque fuselage built of cedar ply laminated around balsa wood. The wing was built as a single unit and the fuselage was then lowered on to it and bolted in place.

Taxiing trials of the prototype, registered G-AEVV, began in May 1937 and the first flight, with R. G. Waight at the controls, was on May 20. Rudder control in the climb was criticised and the original horn-balanced rudders were replaced with end-plate units. The second prototype, G-AEVW, flew in July 1938 but was severely damaged when the fuselage broke in half just aft of the wing following a full-load landing in August. The resulting reinforced fuselage became standard on all production aircraft for Imperial Airways.

First production aircraft to be delivered to the airline was G-AFDI *Frobisher*, which was certificated in October 1938. Others in the "F" Class were 'FDJ *Falcon*, 'FDK *Fortuna*, 'FDL *Fingal* and 'FDM *Fiona*. From November 1938, when scheduled services began, until the outbreak of the Second World War in the following Sep-

tember Albatrosses gave almost trouble-free service on the Croydon to Paris, Brussels and Zurich routes. The fleet was evacuated to Bramcote and later to Whitchurch, from which they operated the Lisbon and Shannon shuttles. The two D.H.91 mailplanes — G-AEVV and 'EVW, named *Faraday* and *Franklin* respectively — were impressed into the RAF in September 1940 to fly the Iceland shuttle. Both of these fine aircraft were destroyed in crashes at Reykjavik in the early years of the war. None of the passenger-carriers was destined to survive the war either; *Frobisher* was destroyed on the ground in December 1940, *Falcon* and *Fiona* were scrapped in September 1943 because of lack of spares, and *Fingal* and *Fortuna* were both destroyed in crashes.

G-AFDI *Frobisher*, **one of five Imperial Airways D.H.91 Albatross airliners**

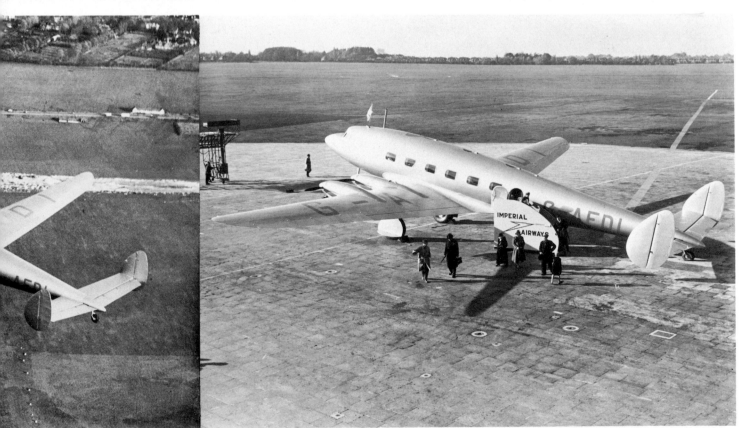

Short-Mayo Composite

The Short-Mayo Composite, a perfectly serious attempt to serve the transatlantic airmail route as efficiently as possible, was the brainchild of Imperial Airways' general manager (technical), Major Robert Mayo. His scheme was to launch a heavily loaded mailplane from the back of a lightly loaded larger aircraft after the combination had climbed to cruising height. The lower component would then return to base to pick up the next mailplane and the cycle would be repeated.

The lower component was an adapted Empire Boat, registered G-ADHK and named *Maia*. It was first flown by J. Lankester Parker on July 27, 1937. The upper component, G-ADHJ *Mercury*, was a clean twin-float seaplane powered by four 340 hp Napier Rapier Vs and capable of a still-air range of 3,800 miles. First flight of *Mercury*, again with Parker in command, was on September 5. Taxiing trials of the Composite began on January 1, 1938, and the first continued flight, with Parker flying *Maia* and Harold Piper in *Mercury*, was on January 20. Handling was satisfactory and on the third flight, on February 6, the first separation was achieved.

After trials at Felixstowe were completed in mid-May and Mercury had been re-engined with Rapier VIs the Composite was handed over to Imperial Airways for fuel-consumption tests. First long-range flight, to Montreal, was on July 21, and an attempt on the seaplane distance record was made by Don Bennett in *Mercury* during August. The outbreak of the Second World War put a stop to further development; *Mercury* was handed over to No 320 (Netherlands) Squadron in June 1940, returning to Felixstowe in August 1941 for disposal. *Maia*, which had been retained for use by BOAC, was destroyed by enemy bombing at her moorings in Poole Harbour in May 1941.

The Short-Mayo Composite, G-ADHJ *Mercury* **and G-ADHK** *Maia*, **assembled for flight**

The Short-Mayo Composite at Rochester

Percival Q6

Designed by Edgar Percival, the handsome twin-engined Q6 light commercial aircraft was built in both fixed and retractable-undercarriage versions. First flight of the prototype, G-AEYE, was made by Percival himself at Luton on September 14, 1937. Some 26 production aircraft were built, the first of which, 'FFD for Sir Philip Sassoon, was delivered in March 1938. Other operators of the fixed-undercarriage version included Lord Londonderry, Intava, Vickers Aviation and H. B. Legge & Sons. First of the retractable-undercarriage Q6s was VH-ABL, built for Australian pilot P. G. Taylor but kept in Britain and re-registered G-AFMT. Q6s were also sold abroad in small numbers, customers including King Ghazi I of Iraq, Tata in India and Hyderabad State Railways.

With the outbreak of the Second World War all British-registered Q6s except for the Vickers aircraft, 'FIW, were impressed for communications duties with the RAF. Seven survived the war and returned to civil life, the longest-lived being 'HOM, which continued flying until July 1958.

Prototype Percival Q6 G-AEYE
Percival Q6 G-AFIX, used by Western Airways Ltd

Armstrong Whitworth A.W.27 Ensign

The four-engined Armstrong Whitworth Ensign was the largest Imperial Airways land-plane to be built before the outbreak of the Second World War. Like its forebear the Atalanta, the Ensign was designed by John Lloyd. Approval for prototype construction was given in September 1934, with delivery set for two years later. A production contract for eleven aircraft was signed on May 29, 1935, with an additional two aircraft ordered in the following

A.W.27 Ensign G-ADSR of Imperial Airways

December. Completion of the first aircraft was delayed by almost two years and the prototype, G-ADSR, did not make its first flight until January 24, 1938. The manufacturer's flight tests were completed in May that year and Imperial Airways' acceptance trials began at the end of June. These trials resulted in the rejection of the prototype, carrying the name *Ensign*, and the second aircraft, *Egeria*, because of the heaviness of the controls and the poor initial rate of climb. Further tests were held during September after Armstrong Whitworth had attended to Imperial Airways' criticisms, and the type entered service on October 20, 1938, when *Ensign* carried 27 passengers from Croydon to Le Bourget. By the end of the year the airline had taken delivery of five A.W.27s, three of which, *Egeria*, *Elsinore* and *Euterpe*, were used on a Christmas mail run to Australia.

Four ''European'' A.W.27s were built. Fitted out for 40 passengers, they were named *Eddystone*, *Ettrick*, *Empyrean* and *Elysian*. By the outbreak of war 11 A.W.27s had been delivered and a few were used initially for ferrying supplies to the British forces in France. These aircraft retained their civilian identity and served with British Overseas Airways Corporation, formed when Imperial Airways merged with British Airways on November 24, 1939.

Three Ensigns were lost flying for National Air Communications: G-ADSZ *Elysian* was destroyed on the ground at Merville, France, on May 23, 1940; 'DTA *Euryalus* was badly damaged in a landing accident at Lympne on the same day; and 'DSX *Ettrick* was badly damaged by bombing at Le Bourget Airport on June 1, 1940. In Britain 'DTC *Endymion* was destroyed by incendiary bombs at Whitchurch on November 24, 1940.

The surviving Ensigns were re-engined with 950 hp Wright Cyclones during 1941 and were joined by the final pair of machines, *Everest* and *Enterprise*; all of these aircraft were designated Ensign Mk II. After modification the aircraft were ferried out to the Middle East and Africa for transport duties with BOAC. They continued to do much useful work and were operating into Calcutta during 1944. At the end of the war they were brought back to Britain for disposal.

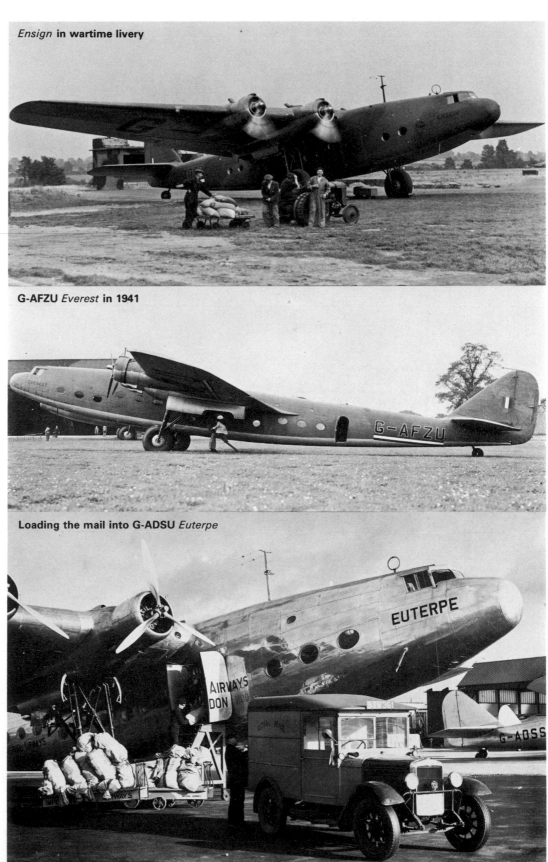

Ensign **in wartime livery**

G-AFZU *Everest* **in 1941**

Loading the mail into G-ADSU *Euterpe*

de Havilland D.H.95 Flamingo

The twin-engined D.H.95 Flamingo, de Havilland's first all-metal stressed-skin aircraft, was designed as a medium-range transport carrying 12 to 17 passengers. Powered by two 890 hp Bristol Perseus XIIC engines, it featured three-bladed variable-pitch propellers, split flaps and hydraulically operated retractable undercarriage.

First flight of the prototype, G-AFUE, was made at Hatfield on December 28, 1938. The generally good performance of the Flamingo attracted the attention of the Air Ministry, which saw it as a 22-seat medium transport. No fewer than 40 were ordered under the designation Hertfordshire, but in the event only one, R2510, was finally built. Total production of the Flamingo ran to only 16 aircraft, 13 of which were placed on civil registers.

Between September 1940 and the following April BOAC took delivery of seven fully camouflaged Flamingoes, all carrying the names of kings of England, for use in the Near East. Three were lost during the war: G-AFYI *King Henry* and 'FYE *King Arthur* in crashes in Turkey and Eritrea respectively, and 'FYG *King Harold* was so badly damaged after its undercarriage collapsed that it was not repaired. The remainder of the BOAC aircraft were grounded through lack of spares by 1944 and were shipped back to Britain and put into temporary storage. After the war all the surviving aircraft were scrapped.

Prototype D.H.95 Flamingo G-AFUE

Short S.26 G-class Flying Boat

The three G-class boats built by Shorts were much larger than the earlier Empire-class boats although they bore a superficial resemblance to them. Powered by four 1,380 hp Bristol Hercules sleeve-valve engines, they were designed to carry a crew of five and some two tons of mail for 2,500 miles. Imperial Airways ordered three G-class boats: G-AFCI *Golden Hind*, 'FCJ *Grenadier* and 'FCK *Grenville*; the last two aircraft were later renamed *Golden Fleece* and *Golden Horn* respectively. *Golden Hind* was the first to be launched, on June 17, 1939, and the first to fly, on July 21. It was handed over to the airline on

Short S.26 *Golden Hind*

Avro 652A Nineteen

Although superficially similar to the earlier Avro 652A Anson 1, the post-war Avro Nineteen was a very different aeroplane, with increased headroom, improved flaps and undercarriage mechanism, and reshaped windows. First civil Nineteen was G-AGNI, ex-MG159. Fitted out with nine passenger seats in 1945, this aircraft was lost off the Isle of Man in June 1948.

Largest operator of Avro Nineteens in the post-war years was Railway Air Services, which used no fewer than 14 on its services from Croydon. After the airline's take-over by BEAC in February 1947 the Avro Nineteens were progressively withdrawn from use.

Towards the end of 1946 a new version of the Anson was made available. Fitted with a new longer-span tapered wing of metal construction, this was the Avro Nineteen Series 2, the first of which was Smiths Instruments' demonstrator, G-AHKX.

Avro 652A Anson G-AMDA of Derby Aviation Ltd

September 24 for crew training, but within a few days all three aircraft had been commandeered by the Royal Air Force.

Two of the G-class boats were lost during the war: *Golden Fleece* force-landed off Cape Finisterre in August 1941 after two engines failed, and *Golden Horn* was lost with 13 occupants in January 1943 after crashing into the Tagus. *Golden Hind* was retired from BOAC service in 1947.

Avro 19 Series 1 G-AHIG of BEA, originally with Railway Air Services

BEA Bristol 170 Mk 1, later acquired by Silver City Airways

Silver City Bristol 170 Mk 32 G-AMWE takes off as Mk 1 G-AGVC lines up

Bristol Type 170 Freighter

Design work on the functional and roomy Type 170 started in 1944, while the Second World War was still in progress, and it was not surprising that the Air Staff seized on this private-venture design, pronouncing it suitable to fill a requirement for a military freighter capable of operating out of rough jungle airstrips in the Far East. Two military prototypes were accordingly ordered to Specifications 22/44 and C.9/45. However, it was soon clear that the war would have ended before the aircraft could reach its theatre of operations, and the design was adapted for civil use by increasing the gross weight and fitting two Bristol Hercules 630 engines.

First flight of the prototype, G-AGPV, was commanded by Cyril Uwins at Filton on December 2, 1945. Two versions of the Type 170 were proposed: the Series 1 or Freighter version, with a specially strengthened floor to carry up to 4½ tons of cargo and hydraulically operated nose doors to accommodate bulky loads or road vehicles; and the Series 2 or Wayfarer, a 32-passenger airliner without the large nose doors. The prototype of this version,

G-AGVB, flew for the first time on April 30, 1945. Chartered to Channel Islands Airways in June 1946, it had carried 10,000 passengers between Croydon and Jersey by the end of October. The first Type 170 to be fully equipped as a Freighter was the third aircraft, G-AGVC, which flew for the first time on June 23, 1946.

The Type 170 was commercially very successful and production totalled more than 200, of which almost 140 were registered to British owners. Probably the best-known operator of the type was cross-Channel ferry operator Silver City Airways, which used no fewer than 32 between July 1948 and July 1956 on its Lympne-Le Touquet route. The airline's need for increased capacity resulted in the introduction of the last variant of the Type 170, the Mark 32. Capable of accommodating 23 passengers and three average-sized cars, the first, G-AMWA, was delivered in March 1953, followed over the next three years by a further 13. The last of Silver City's aircraft, together with those of another large-scale operator, Air Charter Ltd, was consigned to the scrapyard in 1970.

Avro Tudor

The Tudor was not a particularly attractive aeroplane, either to look at or to operate. Derived from the Lincoln bomber, it had the familiar four Merlins on a wing of somewhat greater span, and a new, pressurised fuselage. The prototype, G-AGPF, flew for the first time at Ringway on June 14, 1945. Trials with this aircraft and the second and third prototypes indicated a number of aerodynamic snags, and the original tail unit was greatly modified by the substitution of a taller fin and rudder and a tailplane of greater span. Much of the blame for the Tudor's problems can be laid squarely on the shoulders of BOAC, which was demonstrating that indifferent management and decision-making by committee resulted in compromise and vacillation. Requesting no fewer than 343 modifications, the airline never got the aircraft it wanted and finally abandoned the Tudor altogether in April 1947, cancelling its order for 22 Tudor 1s. Heaping fatal injury upon insult, Tudor 2 prototype G-AGSU crashed, killing designer Roy Chadwick.

Of the 12 production Tudor 1s laid down, two were completed for the Ministry of Supply as Tudor 3 VIP transports with accommodation for nine passengers. The remainder, seating 32 passengers in a lengthened fuselage, were earmarked for British South American Airways and redesignated Tudor 4. Six were delivered but after the mysterious loss of 'HNP *Star Tiger* and 'GRE *Star Ariel* the remainder were relegated to freighting duties. Five 45-seat Tudor 5s also operated by BSAA were reconverted from passenger carriers to fuel tankers and used on the Berlin Airlift during 1948.

BOAC Avro Tudor 1 G-AGRF *Elizabeth of England* **was converted to Tudor 4B standard in 1948**

Tudor 4B G-AHNN *Star Leopard* **of BSAA**

**Avro Tudor 2 prototype G-AGSU (foreground)
with Tudor 1 G-AGRC**

Avro Lancastrian

The Avro Lancastrian was a straightforward transport conversion of the Second World War Lancaster bomber. The first conversion, a Lancaster III, was carried out in Canada during 1943 for Trans-Canada Airlines' transatlantic mail and VIP transport service. The first Avro-built Lancastrian was G-AGLF, ex-VB763, which was handed over to BOAC early in 1945. The corporation ordered 32 modified aircraft but received only 20, the first of which was G-AGLS. Used on the North Atlantic and "Kangaroo" service to Australia, they were far from economical to operate, seating only nine passengers. 1946 saw the appearance of the Lancastrian 3, capable of carrying 13 passengers. This variant was used by British South American Airways on

Lancastrian 3 G-AGWJ *Star Light* **of BSAA. Like G-AGWK, this aircraft crashed in Bermuda in 1947**

services to Buenos Aires and other South American cities, while others were operated by Alitalia, Silver City Airways and Skyways.

During the 1948 Berlin Airlift the Lancastrian was called in as a bulk carrier, ex-BOAC and BSAA aircraft being equipped with large fuselage tanks capable of carrying up to 2,500 gallons.

Avro Lancastrian 3 G-AGWK *Star Trail* **of British South American Airways**

Lancastrian 3 G-AGWG *Star Glow* **crashed in Gambia in 1946**

Avro 685 York G-AGNL *Mersey* of BOAC

Avro York

Originally designed as a military transport for the RAF, the Avro York was a private venture produced in spite of the Anglo-American agreement which compelled the British aircraft industry to neglect transport aircraft development in favour of combat aircraft. (This agree-

ment, incidentally, resulted in a lack of direction from which the industry has never fully recovered.)

Embodying the same wings, engines and twin-fin tail arrangement as the Lancaster bomber, the first military prototype flew for the first time at

Ringway on July 5, 1942. Though volume production did not begin until 1945, the final number of Yorks built exceeded 250, most of them for RAF Transport Command. The first civil aircraft were RAF machines allocated to BOAC for a UK-Cairo cargo and passenger ser-

vice which began in April 1944.

BOAC operated a total of 43 Yorks, including 19 ex-BSAA aircraft acquired after the latter's dissolution in 1949. Many of BOAC's aircraft passed in turn to the independent operator Sky-ways, which had started off with Yorks 'HFI, 'HLV and 'IUP,

York G-AGNX *Moray* **of BOAC**

York G-AGNS *Melville* **of BOAC**

York G-AGSN *Marlow* **of BOAC**

named *Skyway*, *Sky Courier* and
Sky Consul respectively. At one
time or another this airline
owned a total of 37 Yorks.

By the early 1960s the number
of Yorks in scheduled service
had begun to diminish rapidly
and by 1963 most of the British-
registered examples had gone.

de Havilland D.H.104 Dove

This extremely pretty twin-engined feederliner, de Havilland's post-war Rapide replacement, was originally fitted out for eight passengers and a crew of two. Conforming to the Brabazon Committee's Specification 5B, the Dove was of conventional all-metal construction and was powered by two de Havilland Gipsy Queen 71 engines. The prototype, G-AGPJ, flew for the first time at Hatfield on September 25, 1945, and was thus the first British civil transport to fly after the end of the Second World War.

The Dove got off to an unfortunate start when two early aircraft were lost in fatal crashes: G-AGUC in August 1946 and 'HRA in March 1947. It was also expensive to buy and operate, and under-capitalised British charter operators, often staffed by otherwise unemployable ex-RAF transport and bomber aircrew, were unable to pay the high costs involved. Nevertheless, around 540 of the type were built, with the majority going abroad.

American companies produced two interesting versions, both radical conversions of existing Dove airframes. The first, by Riley Aeronautics, featured a restyled flight deck and cabin, a new swept fin, and a pair of 400 hp Lycoming IO-720s in place of the Gipsy Queens. Called the Riley Turbo Exec 400, it enjoyed only limited success, production running to just 17 examples. The other hybrid was a slightly more ambitious project known as the Carstedt CJ-600A Jet Liner, which first flew in December 1966. This conversion involved a substantial fuselage stretch to increase passenger capacity to 18, and the use of a pair of 605 hp Garrett AiResearch turboprops.

Dove 1 CC-CLW of Linea Aerea Nacional, Chile

Handley Page Hermes

The first new British aircraft to enter service with BOAC after the Second World War, the four-engined pressurised Handley Page Hermes had its origins in a wartime specification calling for a 34/50-passenger airliner with a crew of seven. The prototype, G-AGSS, was destroyed shortly after take-off on its maiden flight, on December 3, 1945, and the development effort was switched temporarily to the Hermes' military counterpart, the Hastings troop transport.

However, in April 1947 BOAC ordered 25 tricycle-undercarriage Hermes 4s, the first of which, G-AKFP, flew for the first time in September 1948. Some 13 feet longer than the ill-fated Hermes 1, the new aircraft accommodated up to 63 passengers and seven crew and first entered service with BOAC in August 1950 on the West African route. Regarded as interim aircraft only, BOAC's Hermes were gradually replaced by Argonauts and the first of the surplus aircraft were acquired by Airwork in 1952 for military trooping charters. Other independent British operators included Air Safaris, Falcon Airways, Skyways and Silver City.

The type was gradually withdrawn from service from 1958 and the majority were scrapped at Hurn and Stansted during 1961 and 1962. The last commercial Hermes flight was made by Air Links' 'LDA in 1964.

Hermes 4 G-ALDI of BOAC carries on the name *Hannibal*

D.H.104 Dove VR-NIB

Handley Page H.P.81 Hermes 4 G-ALDM *Hero* **of BOAC**

Handley Page Halton

Like the Avro Lancaster, the Halifax bomber was subjected to a crude "civilianisation" at the end of the Second World War in an attempt to establish a large-scale passenger and freight network equal to that existing just before the war. Less successful than the Lancastrian, the Handley Page conversion nevertheless provided operators with a workable interim solution.

First conversion was G-AGXA *Waltzing Matilda*, which left Hurn on May 26, 1946, en route to Australia. A total of 147 conversions ultimately appeared on the British register, with two of the largest fleets belonging to Dr Graham Humby's London Aero and Motor Services and the Lancashire Aircraft Company.

Useful though the early Halifax conversions were, the Halifax C.VIII adaptation, known as the Halton, offered more payload. Twelve Haltons were produced from July 1946, beginning with G-AHDU *Falkirk*, and all were allocated to BOAC. With accommodation for ten passengers and up to 8,000lb of assorted freight in the under-fuselage pannier, the Halton was put to work on routes to West Africa, Cairo and Karachi. Like the Hermes, the Halton was withdrawn from service with the introduction of the Canadair Argonauts, although many received a new, if brief, lease of life during the Berlin Airlift.

Handley Page H.P.70 Halton G-AHDU *Falkirk* of BOAC

Miles M.65 Gemini 1A G-AGUS

Vickers Viking

The hint of Wellington bomber about the Viking was no accident. Designed by Rex Pierson towards the end of the Second World War to fulfil a requirement for a "Wellington Transport Aircraft", the Viking prototype did in fact incorporate the geodetic outer wing panels, engine nacelles and landing gear of that famous bomber. Seating was provided for 21 passengers and four crew in a cigar-shaped stressed-skin fuselage. Prototype G-AGOK was flown for the first time by Mutt Summers at Wisley on June 22, 1945, and the type was issued with its certificate of airworthiness in the following April.

Vickers built 19 Viking 1As, 11 of which were delivered to BEA during 1946. Production continued with 31 Viking 1s, which featured conventional stressed-skin wings; most of these aircraft were also delivered to BEA. By the time production ended in 1947, 48 "short-nosed" and 113 "long-nosed" Vikings had been built. A good many of the long-nosed Viking 1Bs were sold abroad to operators in Africa, South America, the Middle East and Europe. As the major airlines began to re-equip with more modern aircraft Vikings became available in increasing numbers for sale to smaller charter carriers, and many continued to fly right up to the end of the 1960s. None remained in service by 1974.

Vickers Type 610 Viking 1B G-AJBR *Sir Bertram Ramsay*

Miles Gemini and Aries

The prototype Gemini was little more than a standard Messenger airframe fitted with two 100 hp Cirrus Minor engines. It was flown for the first time by George Miles at Woodley on October 26, 1945. Acclaimed as being delightful to fly, the Gemini quickly entered series production and the first demonstration machine, G-AIDO, was certificated in August 1946. Some 170 Geminis and two of the 155 hp Blackburn Cirrus Major-engined Aries were built, 130 of them in the first year. Most eventually found their way abroad. Operators included *Flight* magazine, the Goodyear Tyre and Rubber Co,

the Arab Contracting and Trading Co and the Missionary Aviation Fellowship, whose G-AKZK crashed in the Belgian Congo in July 1948.

Last of the Gemini variants was the M.75 Aries, which flew for the first time in February 1951. Apart from engines of increased power, the Aries had a strengthened airframe and larger vertical tail than that of the standard Gemini. Both examples left Britain: 'MDJ, the prototype, was re-registered VH-FAV on its arrival in Australia in 1954, and 'OGA, after spending several years at White Waltham, was dispatched to Ireland with the registration EI-ANB.

Type 635 Viking 1B G-AMGG *Sir Robert Calder*, **ex-ZS-BNE**

Miles Aerovan

Designed in 1944 as a short-range freighter, the wooden M.57 Aerovan could carry eight passengers or a ton of cargo for up to 450 miles on the power of two 310 hp Cirrus Major 3 engines. The prototype flew for the first time on January 26, 1945, carrying the identification U-0248. Later registered G-AGOZ, it was sold to Western Mfg Estates in 1948 and scrapped at Woodley in the following year. Production Aerovans had the front fuselage extended by 18in and were fitted with round portholes in place of the square windows of the prototype. Miles built seven Mk III Aerovans, all identical to the single Mk II, G-AGWO, except for a heavy-duty lock on the rear fuselage door. Five were used by Air Contractors of Blackbushe on a cross-Channel freight service. Main production version was the Mk IV, of which 41 were built; two others were left uncompleted. Two Mk IVs joined Air Contractors' Mk IIIs, four were ferried out to Spain for use by Aerotechnica SA, and others were operated by such charter companies as Air Transport (Charter) of Jersey, Channel Islands, East Anglian Flying Services, and North Sea Air Transport Ltd of Brough. Largest user was Ulster Aviation of Newtownards, which operated five over a three-year period between 1947 and 1949.

Two Mk VIs were built: G-AJOF, fitted in January 1955 with an experimental high-aspect-ratio wing of Hurel-Dubois design and re-registered G-AHDM; and G-AKHF, sold in Italy during 1954 and re-registered I-VALK.

Miles M.57 Aerovan Mk IV G-AILF

Aerovan Mk IV G-AJOB of Ulster Aviation Ltd

This four-engined development of the Aerovan, the M.71 Merchantman, was scrapped in 1948

Short S.25 Sandringham 7 G-AKCO *St George* **of BOAC**

Short S.25 Sandringham 2 G-AGPZ, later LV-AAO *Argentina*

Short Sunderland 3 and Sandringham

In December 1942 six RAF Short Sunderland 3s were taken from the production line at Rochester, stripped of their military equipment and armament and fitted with bench seats. At the beginning of 1943 they were given civil markings and put to work by BOAC on the Poole to West Africa run. At the end of the war in Europe the Sunderlands were divested of their camouflage and re-engined with more powerful Pegasus 38s; their interiors were also modified to carry 24 day or 16 sleeper passengers and 6,500lb of freight. First to be refurbished was G-AGJM, named *Hythe*, which later became the class name for all of the conversions. BOAC converted 18 at Hythe, and Short a further four at Belfast in readiness for the opening of the new Empire routes to the Far East and Australia in January 1946.

Before that, in 1945, one of the original Sunderland 3 conversions had been returned to Rochester to have its nose and tail remodelled to resemble

those of the old Empire boats. It re-emerged on November 28, 1945, as the first Sandringham I. Named *Himalaya*, it offered the same accommodation as the *Hythe* boats. Short was hoping that BOAC would adopt the Sandringham as its standard Empire route boat, but the first order came in fact from the Argentine operator Dodero of Buenos Aires. Designated Sandringham 2, these aircraft were named *Argentina*, *Uruguay* and *Paraguay* and were ferried out to their new owner in British markings. Dodero also took possession of two Sandringham 3s, *Brazil* and *Inglaterra*.

Other orders for Sandringhams came from Tasman Empire Airways, which needed four to replace its ageing Empire Flying Boats. Designated Sandringham 4, they were named *Tasman*, *Australia*, *New Zealand* and *Auckland*. The first of these, fitted out for 30 day passengers, was delivered in July 1946.

Delays in delivery of its new landplanes forced BOAC to

reconsider its refusal to buy Sandringhams, and in 1947 the airline leased from the Ministry of Civil Aviation nine Twin Wasp-powered Sandringham 5s named *Portsmouth*, *Perth*, *Penzance*, *Portland*, *Pembroke*, *Portmarnock*, *Portsea*, *Poole* and *Pevensey*. Beginning operations in May 1947, they relieved the Hythes on the routes between Poole and Sydney, Hong Kong and Bahrain, and between Sydney and Singapore.

The following year BOAC ordered a further three improved boats. Designated Sandringham 7 and known as the Bermuda class, they were fitted out for 30 passengers. Named *Saint George*, *Saint David* and *Saint Andrew*, they were flown regularly by BOAC between 1948 and 1950. After the corporation had changed over to landplanes the large BOAC fleet was widely dispersed, most of the Sunderland 3s going to Aquila Airways while the Sandringhams were either scrapped or sold abroad.

Sandringham 7 flight deck

Short Solent

Early in 1946 BOAC was given the opportunity to evaluate the second production Seaford 1, temporarily registered G-AGWU. Larger than the Sunderland, it was felt to have more potential for conversion to airliner standard. The corporation ordered 12, each powered by Bristol Hercules 637s and fitted out for 30 passengers on two decks. Designated Short Solent 2 and carrying the registrations G-AHIL to 'HIY (less 'HIP and 'HIQ, which were not allocated), they were named *Salisbury*, *Scarborough*, *Southampton*, *Somerset*, *Sark*, *Scapa*, *Severn*, *Solway*, *Salcombe*, *Stornoway*, *Sussex* and *Southsea*.

The first of these, 'HIL *Salisbury*, was launched on November 11, 1946, and the last, 'HIY *Southsea*, on April 8, 1948; *Southsea* was the last aircraft ever to be built at Rochester.

The Solent 2s were owned by the Ministry of Civil Aviation and leased to BOAC, and in order to give the corporation its own air-

Short S.45 Solent 2 G-AHIS *Scapa* **of BOAC**

craft it was decided in 1948 to acquire the six Seaford 1s under construction at Belfast and have them completed as Solent 3s. They were fitted out for 39 passengers and the first, G-AKNO, was named *City of London* on May 5, 1949. In fact only four were registered to BOAC, the other three being 'KNP *City of Cardiff*, 'KNR *City of Belfast* and 'KNS *City of Liverpool*.

When the BOAC flying-boat fleet disbanded in November 1950 most of the Solents were scrapped at Hamworthy or Belfast, although 'HIO *Somerset* and 'HIV *Salcombe* were sold to Trans-Oceanic Airways of Sydney in 1951.

Solent 3 G-ANAJ *City of Funchal* **of Aquila Airways**

Solent G-AHIU *Solway* **of BOAC**

Solent 4 G-AOBL *Aotearoa II* of Aquila Airways

Handley Page Marathon

The Marathon was designed by Miles Aircraft Ltd to meet the Brabazon Committee's Specifications 5a and 18/44 for a feederliner for British internal networks. First flown as U-10 on May 19, 1946, the prototype had a triple-finned tail, as did the production aircraft, though the second prototype, G-AILH, was flown with a twin-finned assembly. Powered by four 330 hp de Havilland Gipsy Queens, it could carry a crew of two and up to 20 passengers and looked set fair for a degree of commercial success. Problems fell thick and fast, however, starting with the financial difficulties suffered by the manufacturer during 1947 and 1948 and compounded by the loss of the prototype, G-AGPD, in a fatal crash at Boscombe Down in May 1948.

In 1948 Miles Aircraft went into liquidation and the company's assets were taken over by Handley Page in June of that year. Named Handley Page (Reading) Ltd, the new HP subsidiary was charged with continuing Marathon development and production. The new designation was HPR 1 and orders at that time stood at 40 aircraft for BEA. First production aircraft was 'LUB, which left Woodley in January 1950 on a sales tour to New Zealand. BEA, meanwhile, was having second thoughts about the type's suitability as a Rapide replacement and had cut its order to only seven aircraft. In February 1952 the airline finally abandoned the Marathon and 30 were diverted by the Ministry of Supply to the RAF as T.11 advanced navigation trainers.

Of the remainder, six were supplied to West African Airways in 1952, three to Burma Airways, two to Far East Airlines and one in 1954 to King Hussein of Jordan.

**Second prototype
Miles M.60 Marathon 1 G-AILH**

Handley Page (Reading) HPR 1 Marathon G-ALUB

Mamba-powered Miles M.60 Marathon 2 G-AHXU

Prototype Airspeed AS.65 Consul G-AGVY, a converted RAF Oxford

Consul MC-ABA for Monte Carlo Airways. The aircraft was not delivered

Airspeed AS.65 Consul

The Airspeed AS.65 Consul was essentially a civilianised version of the RAF Oxford twin-engined trainer. Between 1946 and 1948 more than 150 airframes were converted at Airspeed's Portsmouth factory. Main structural alterations were the provision of extra windows for the six passengers, a longer nose with access to the forward baggage hold, and a partition between the cabin and flight deck, and re-setting of the tailplane to permit a forward movement of the centre of gravity.

First of the conversions was G-AGVY, certificated in March 1946 and delivered to the Bata Shoe Co. Because it was a conversion of a military-surplus type Airspeed was able to put an attractive price tag on the Consul, and it was bought in relatively large quantities by 11 or 12 British operators. Consuls were also sold abroad in significant numbers, particularly in French Indo-China, the Near East and French colonial Africa.

Airspeed AS.57 Ambassador

Built to conform to the Brabazon Committee's Requirement IIA for a European short-haul airliner, Specification 25/43, the Ambassador was a twin-engined high-wing aircraft accommodating between 28 and 50 passengers, depending on configuration. The prototype, G-AGUA, flew for the first time at Christchurch on July 10, 1947, and almost immediately impressed the public with its graceful, modern lines and comfortable passenger cabin.

An order for 20 was received from BEA in September 1948, the airline specifying the Centaurus 661 with two-stage supercharger in place of the prototype's Centaurus 130s. The first production aircraft, G-AMAD, flew for the first time in January 1951 and, together with production prototype 'LFR, was soon undergoing intensive proving trials. Flagship of the new Elizabethan class was G-ALZN, delivered to BEA at Heathrow on August 22, 1951. First scheduled service was flown on March 13, 1952, to Paris and it soon became apparent that the Ambassador had better operating costs than any other BEA aircraft, particularly on shorter sectors.

BEA began replacing its Ambassador fleet during 1957, the first three aircraft to be released going to Australian carrier Butler Air Transport Ltd. They returned to Britain in 1958 and the following year were sold

Prototype AS.57 Ambassador G-AGUÄ in August 1947

Autair Ambassador 2 G-ALZZ, ex-BEA *Edmund Spenser*

to Dan-Air, together with five other ex-BEA aircraft, for operation from Gatwick on charters and inclusive tours until 1968. Other British-based operators included BKS Air Transport Ltd, which flew its Ambassadors on Newcastle-Dublin, and Autair International Airways, which used three 'LZS, 'LZV and 'LZZ, between 1963 and 1968.

Ambassador 2 G-ALZS *William Shakespeare* **of BEA**

Dan-Air Ambassador 2 G-ALZO, ex-BEA *Christopher Marlow*

Bristol 171 Sycamore

The four-seat Bristol 171 Mk 1 was designed by Austrian-born Raoul Hafner, wartime director of the Airborne Forces Experimental Establishment rotorcraft team. Powered by a 450 hp Pratt & Whitney Wasp Junior, the prototype flew for the first time at Filton on July 27, 1947. The second prototype, G-ALOU, received its certificate of airworthiness in January 1949, thereby becoming the first British helicopter to be certificated.

Only one Mk 2, VW905, was built. Powered by a 550 hp Alvis Leonides engine, it first flew in September 1949 but never took up its civil registration. The five-seat Mk 3 had a shorter nose for improved forward view and was the first Sycamore to enter series production. Only two retained British civil registrations: G-ALSR *Sir Gareth*, loaned to BEA for evaluation, and 'LSX, the company demonstrator. Two others, designated Mk 3A and with an extra freight hold located aft of the engine bay, were completed for BEA. G-AMWG *Sir Gawain* and 'MWH *Sir Geraint* were used on an experimental Eastleigh-Heathrow/Northolt service from June 1954; 'MWG was sold to Ansett-ANA in 1956.

A very small number of Mk 4s were also allotted civil markings, including 'MWI, used for airborne television experiments in 1956, and 'ODL, sold to Australian National Airways as VH-INO.

Bristol Type 171 Mk 3A G-AMWG, leased to BEA as *Sir Gawain*

Cunliffe-Owen Concordia

The Concordia was a conventional twin-engined medium-range transport designed by W. Garrow-Fisher and built by Cunliffe-Owen Aircraft at Eastleigh, near Portsmouth. Only two examples of this tricycle-undercarriage ten-seater were built: prototype Y-0222 was first flown at Eastleigh by A. Corbin in May 1947, while the second aircraft, G-AKBE, was shown at the SBAC Show at Radlett in the same year.

During 1947 a production batch of six was laid down, one of which, G-AKBF/VT-CQT, was earmarked for the Nawab of Bhopal, with two more for BEA. Work was suspended in November 1947 when it was decided that there was insufficient market interest to justify further investment.

Prototype Cunliffe-Owen Concordia Y-0222

Percival Prince

The twin-engined, shoulder-wing Prince was derived from the similarly configured P.48 Merganser, which flew for the first time on May 9, 1947, as X-2. Later registered G-AHMH, it was flown extensively to gather data for the production Prince before being scrapped at Luton in August 1948.

The P.50 Prince was much larger than the Merganser, weighing over 3,000lb more and fitted with engines practically twice as powerful as the earlier aircraft's 296 hp Gipsy Queen 51s. The prototype, G-23-1, later registered G-ALCM, flew for the first time at Luton on May 13, 1948. An initial batch of ten production aircraft was laid down during 1948 and the first production Prince 1, G-ALFZ, was despatched on a long proving flight to the Cape in March 1949.

Successive versions of the basic Prince were fitted with more powerful Alvis Leonides engines, each conferring slightly better performance. The ultimate version was the Prince 5, later known as the President, which had the longer-span wing of the military Pembroke and nacelles modified at the back to improve single-engine handling. First flown in August 1956, the prototype, G-AOJG, was later sold to the Danish AF.

Prototype P.48 Merganser X2, later registered G-AHMH

P.50 Prince G-ALRY of Hunting Aerosurveys Ltd

Short Sealand

The Short Sealand, designed by C. T. P. Lipscomb, was the company's last water-based aircraft. The prototype, G-AIVX, flew for the first time from Belfast Lough on January 22, 1948, and shortly afterwards the manufacturer laid down a production batch of Sealand 1s.

The first of 14 British-registered aircraft, G-AKLM, was destroyed in October 1949 during a sales tour of Scandinavia. Three aircraft ordered by British West Indian Airways were not delivered when it was discovered that they were expected to operate from completely unsuitable bases, and they were diverted instead to the manufacturer or to Jugoslovenski Aero Transport.

No Sealand 2s were built; this projected variant was to have been powered by a pair of Alvis Leonides radials. Sealand 3 was the designation given to two examples operated by Norwegian carrier Vestlandske Luftfartselskap; these aircraft had their wheeled undercarriage removed. Other operators included the East Bengal Transport Commission, which acquired G-AKLX and 'KLY in late 1952, and Ralli Bros in East Pakistan, which used ex-G-AKLV *Pegasus* as AP-AFM.

Short Sealand 6 G-AKLO

Vickers Viscount 630 prototype G-AHRF in BEA colours

Vickers Viscount series

The Viscount series of airliners was one of the few commercially successful aircraft programmes to emerge from Britain after the Second World War. Derived from a Vickers proposal for a four-engined version of the Viking, the design was modified to meet the specification laid down in the Brabazon Committee's Requirement IIB for a pressurised 24-seater. The Ministry of Supply later ordered two prototypes of a larger, 32-seat aircraft from Vickers, the Armstrong Siddeley Mamba-powered Type 609 Viceroy. A third prototype was to be financed by the manufacturer. It was later decided to re-engine the Ministry prototypes with Rolls-Royce Darts, and G-AHRF and 'HRG were redesignated Type 630 and named Viscount. First flight of 'HRF was made at Wisley on July 16, 1948.

Shortly after, the availability of uprated Dart engines allowed the manufacturer to propose a higher-capacity aircraft which more closely met the requirements of BEA. An order for a prototype of this 43-seat aircraft, the Viscount 700, was placed in February 1949. Seating capacity was later increased to 53 and the production version, designated the Viscount 701, was launched with a BEA order for 27 aircraft. First of the production aircraft, G-ALWE, first flew in August 1952 and, named *Wisley*, became the flagship of the new Discovery class. By the time the first of these entered service with BEA in April 1953 substantial orders had been received

from other carriers, including Air France, Aer Lingus and TCA. The TCA order was significant in that it represented the first of many to be received from the lucrative North American market. Later named Air Canada, TCA was at the time the largest operator of Series 700 Viscounts.

In February 1953 BEA ordered 12 larger Viscounts powered by yet more powerful Dart turboprops. This 86-passenger version was designated Viscount 801 and was to have been more than 13ft longer than the basic 701. The stretch was thought to be too great, however, and the definitive aircraft, the Type 802, emerged as a 65-seater with the stretch confined to 3ft 10in. First flown in July 1956, the first of the 24 eventually delivered to BEA entered service the following February. BEA also ordered 19 Type 806s in 1956. More significant was the new Viscount 810 then under construction, which embodied structural and aerodynamic advances over the earlier aircraft. This series, evolved originally to meet a requirement of US carrier Continental Airlines, was built in large numbers for a wide variety of customers in almost every continent.

Viscount production had virtually ceased at the end of 1959 after a total of more than 450 aircraft had been built. It seems likely that examples of this most successful of pioneering turbo-prop airliners will continue to fly in all parts of the world for years to come.

Viscount 700 prototype G-AMAV in BEA colours

BRITISH EUROPEAN AIRWAYS

G-AMAV

Viscount 803 PH-VID *Otto Lilienthal* **of KLM**

Viscount 806 G-AOYS *George Stephenson* **of BEA**

OLLANDER

KLM

Viscount 769 CX-AQN of PLUNA

VISCOUNT

CX-AQN

*P*rimeras *L*ineas *U*ruguas de *N*avigacion *A*ereá

PLUNA

Armstrong Whitworth Apollo

Like the Vickers Viscount, the Mamba-powered Armstrong Whitworth A.W.55 Apollo was designed to meet the Brabazon Committee Requirement IIB for a 24-seat European transport. Construction of two prototypes began early in 1948, with a third airframe earmarked for ground testing. Carrying RAF markings and the serial VX220, the first prototype flew for the first time on April 10, 1949. Apart from problems with the Mamba engines there were also short-comings in control and stability which necessitated modifications to the tail assembly. These completed, the aircraft was given the civil registration G-AIYN and attempts to sell this doomed aircraft began. But in June 1952 it was decided to abandon further development of the Apollo; the second aircraft, VX224, had still to fly at that stage.

Having no commercial future, the two aircraft were handed over to the Aeroplane and Armament Experimental Establishment at Boscombe Down. G-AIYN was scrapped at Baginton in 1955 and VX224 (which never carried its allotted civil registration, G-AMCH) was dismantled at Farnborough in 1957 after serving without distinction at the Empire Test Pilots' School for less than a year.

Armstrong Whitworth A.W.55 Apollo G-AIYN

Prototype Bristol Type 167 Brabazon G-AGPW in July 1951

Brabazon G-AGPW during 1950

Bristol Brabazon

Bristol's mammoth Brabazon should never have been built; it was a waste of design effort and a waste of materials. As its name suggests, the Brabazon was born of one of the Brabazon Committee's wartime proposals, this time for an aircraft capable of carrying an economical load over London-New York distances.

Detailed design work was well under way by the end of 1944 and the first manufacturing drawings were issued in April 1945, with construction beginning that October. The prototype, G-AGPW, was finally rolled out at Filton in January 1949, by which time it was obvious that the programme was running less than smoothly. The much heralded first flight was continually postponed and did not take place until September 4. The second Brabazon, allocated the registration G-AIML, was never completed and the programme was suspended in 1952. Both airframes were broken up in 1953.

Brabazon G-AGPW during 1950

D.H.106 Comet 1 G-ALYP of BOAC, destroyed by explosive decompression in January 1954

The only Comet 3, G-ANLO, in BEA livery

de Havilland D.H.106 Comet series

Development work on the Comet was started by de Havilland as early as 1944 and proceeded along the lines suggested by the Brabazon Committee's Type IV requirement, although the company was confident that it could achieve better performance than that called for by the specification. Co-operation with BOAC headed the company away from one or two of the more bizarre solutions that it had been nursing, among them twin-boom and tailless configurations, and design effort was concentrated on a more orthodox layout. The Ministry of Supply ordered two prototypes to Specification 22/46, and the project was named Comet in December 1947.

The first prototype, G-5-1 (later registered G-ALVG), was flown for the first time by John Cunningham on July 27, 1949, at which time the design had crystallised as a 36-seat aircraft. The second aircraft, G-ALZK, flew for the first time exactly a year later and was delivered to BOAC's Comet unit at Hurn in April 1951. The airline had nine Comet 1s on order at that time, all of which were delivered between early 1951 and September 1952. The first scheduled service, to Johannesburg, took place in May 1952 and was notable as being the first flight by a jet carrying farepaying passengers.

Although fast, comfortable and economical to operate, the early Comets were to suffer from a series of puzzling fatal accidents which would have seriously jeopardised future development if the Accidents Investigation Branch at Farnborough had not succeeded in pinpointing the exact cause: metal fatigue and consequent structural failure.

Slightly longer than the Comet 1, the Mk 2 was powered by more powerful Rolls-Royce Avon 503s and had its fuel capacity increased by 1,000 gallons, increasing the range. In addition to the modified Comet 1 airframe, G-ALYT, de Havilland built twelve British-registered Mk 2s, all but four of which were diverted to the RAF.

Only one Comet 3, G-ANLO, was built. Powered by Avon 523s and configured for 78 passengers, it was developed into the Comet 4. This stretched aircraft — now more than 15ft longer than the Comet 2 — met BOAC's requirement for a transatlantic airliner and the airline ordered 19. The first of these, G-APDA, first flew in April 1958. Its sister aircraft, 'PDB and 'PDC, were the first commercial jets across the North Atlantic, one westbound and the other eastbound, in October 1958, beating Pan Am's Boeing 707s by just three weeks.

Successive developed versions were the Comet 4B and 4C. The former was stretched by a further 6ft 6in to 118ft and carried up to 99 passengers in tourist configuration. The latter combined the longer-span wing of the basic Comet 4 with the new stretched fuselage.

Hatfield-built Comet 4 G-APDA of BOAC

Chester-built Comet 4C G-AROV on lease to Middle East Airlines

de Havilland D.H.114 Heron

This Dove development was first flown at Hatfield on May 10, 1950, carrying the registration G-ALZL. The Heron Mk 1 was powered by four 250 hp de Havilland Gipsy Queen 30s and featured a fixed tricycle undercarriage. Accommodation was provided for up to 17 passengers and a crew of two. The first production aircraft was ZK-AYV for New Zealand National Airways, delivered in April 1952. Total production of Heron 1s amounted to 52 aircraft, including the prototype; only seven of these were built at Hatfield, the remainder coming off the Chester line.

The Heron 2's fully retractable undercarriage significantly improved performance and the type soon found favour as a luxury executive transport, customers including Anglo-American Corporation of South Africa, the Governor-General of the Belgian Congo and the Queen's Flight. The type also served with several airlines all over the world, including the Turkish carrier Devlet Hava Yollari, which had seven Herons, Indian Airlines, West African Airways and many others.

Like the Dove, the Heron was extensively modified by such companies as Riley and Saunders. The Riley Turbo-Skyliner was a re-engined Heron powered by four 290 hp supercharged Lycomings giving the aircraft a maximum speed of 285 mph, while the Saunders ST-27 was essentially a remanufactured aircraft, stretched by more than ten feet and powered by a pair of PT6A-34 turboprops.

D.H.114 Heron 1 G-ANXA Sister Joan Kennedy of BEA subsidiary Scottish Airways

Heron 2 TC-HAK of Turkish Airlines

Heron 2 G-ANCJ in 1956

Bristol 173

The Bristol 173 was a 13-passenger helicopter powered by two Leonides Majors driving tandem rotors. The first prototype, G-ALBN, made its first hovering flight on January 3, 1952. The second prototype, G-AMJI, was fitted with a revised undercarriage with castoring front wheels and fixed rear wheels and had small stub wings fore and aft, with winglets on the tips of the aft wings. After naval trials this aircraft was lent for operational trials to BEA, which named it *Sir Bors*. Three Bristol 173 Mk 3s, with four-bladed rotors and taller aft pylons, were to have been built for civil use. But they were in fact completed for the Ministry of Supply and carried RAF serials. One of the three, XE288, was later allocated a second civil registration, G-AORB, and painted in BEA livery, but it never progressed beyond the ground-running stage.

Bristol 173 Mk 2 G-AMJI in BEA livery

Bristol Type 175 Britannia Series 103 G-ANBC of BOAC

Bristol Britannia series

The Type 175 Britannia was Bristol's response to a 1947 BOAC requirement for a medium-range Empire transport. In its earliest form it was a Centaurus-powered 32/36-passenger aircraft. But since the engines were more powerful than was necessary for the specified payload it was decided to increase the gross weight and thus the passenger capacity to 40 or 44, depending on configuration. In July 1948 the Ministry of Supply ordered three prototypes of the Centaurus-powered aircraft, the second and third prototypes to be suitable for conversion to Proteus gas turbines. Having taken a positive interest in the Proteus-engined version in October

1948, BOAC finally signed a contract for 25 in the following July, by which time the design had crystallised as an 83-seat aircraft capable of transatlantic operation at a gross weight of 130,000lb.

Only two prototypes, G-ALBO and 'LRX, were actually built, the third airframe becoming the functional mock-up. 'LBO first flew at Filton on August 16, 1952, powered by four Proteus 625s. These engines were later changed for the definitive aircraft's Proteus 705s, rated at 3,780 eshp. After a large amount of development flying the corporation put its Britannia 102s to work on the Johannesburg route from February 1957, and on services to Australia during

the following month. Of the initial order for 25 Britannias, 15 were completed as 102s and the other ten were reserved for completion in the form of a projected higher-capacity version. The first of these stretched aircraft were designated Britannia 300 and, powered by Proteus 755s, could carry up to 99 tourist-class passengers. First flight of the prototype Britannia 301 took place in July 1956, by which time overseas interest in this variant had increased. BOAC relinquished its claim to the Mk 302s under construction, which were then delivered to Aeronaves de Mexico, Transcontinental SA, Air Charter and Ghana Airways. BOAC's major order for improved Britannias

covered 18 Mk 312s. Deliveries began in September 1957 and transatlantic services started in December of that year.

Other customers for 300-series aircraft included El Al, which had four Mk 313s, Canadian Pacific with six Mk 314s, Hunting Clan and Cubana. Final version was the 4,445 ehp Proteus 765-powered Series 324, of which just two were completed for Canadian Pacific; these aircraft later passed into the hands of British Eagle as G-ARKA and 'RKB. This airline acquired a good proportion of the BOAC fleet, which had been retired in 1965. By the mid-1970s almost all of the long-range Britannias had been withdrawn from airline use.

The only Britannia Series 301, G-ANCA, crashed in November 1957

Britannia Series 312 G-AOVK of BOAC

El Al Britannia at Farnborough

Saro Princess flying boat G-ALUN

Saro Princess

The Saro Princess was a vain and ill-conceived attempt to repeat the pre-war success of the Empire Flying Boats by marrying an old idea to new technology. Although first flown in 1952 and surviving until 1967, the Princess spent almost the whole of that time quietly rotting at Calshot.

Ordered by Minister of Supply George Strauss for BOAC in May 1946, the three boats were registered G-ALUN, 'LUO and 'LUP. First flight of 'LUN was commanded by Geoffrey Tyson on August 22, 1952. But by this time technology had long since moved on, particularly in the field of engines, and work was suspended on the second and third airframes while the Government, Saro and Bristol tried to agree on how to install Bristol's new Orion turboprop. No agreement was forthcoming and all three aircraft were cocooned, 'LUN having flown only a handful of hours. Over the next ten years a number of possible buyers emerged, but none took delivery of the aircraft and by 1967 all had been scrapped.

G-ALUN on the slipway at Cowe

Princess flying boat at Farnborough in 1952

Scottish Aviation Twin Pioneer

The prototype Twin Pioneer, G-ANTP, flew for the first time at Prestwick on June 25, 1955. Designed to carry up to 16 passengers and a crew of two, it was an unpretentious STOL transport powered by a pair of 540 hp Alvis Leonides engines. With its outstanding short-field performance and modest operating costs, the Twin Pioneer appeared to have extremely good sales potential and the manufacturer planned production of 200 aircraft. During 1957 the type was despatched on a number of intensive sales tours. After an appearance at the 1957 Paris Show, G-AOEO was lost on its way to South Africa, crashing at Tripoli in December 1957 and killing Scottish Aviation managing director D. F. McIntyre and Capt Roy Smith. Production continued, however, and a total of 85 were built in addition to the two prototypes; 39 Twin Pioneers went to the RAF.

The 33rd aircraft, G-APPW, was completed as a Series 2, powered by two 600 hp Pratt & Whitney R-1340 radials, in response to an order from Philippine Air Lines for five similarly powered examples. At the peak of its career the Twin Pioneer was operating with 15 carriers in 20 countries. Several of these aircraft had been converted from Series 1 to Series 3 standard, their early Alvis Leonides 514s having been replaced with more powerful 640 hp Leonides 531s.

The type was particularly suited to such duties as photographic and geophysical survey; in the latter role it carried the transmitting and receiving aerials in wingtip fairings. Rio Tinto Zinc's Series 1 G-AOER was one such aircraft.

Scottish Aviation Twin Pioneer at Farnborough

Twin Pioneer VR-OAE of Borneo Airways before delivery

Fairey Rotodyne prototype

Fairey Rotodyne

The Rotodyne was conceived to meet BEA's requirement for a "Bealine Bus" multi-engined helicopter, amongst other things. This called for a 30-passenger city-to-city commuter aircraft. Fairey elected to develop a compound helicopter powered by two turboprop engines and rotor-tip jets. The prototype, carrying RAF serial number XE521, flew for the first time on November 6, 1957. Early flights were all made in the helicopter mode, the first transition to and from autogyro mode

being made on April 18, 1958.

It had been confidently expected that BEA would order the Rotodyne once the military had itself signed a contract, but in early 1956 budget cuts signalled a cooling in RAF and Army interest, although the project was still being funded by the Ministry of Defence. A breakthrough seemed to have been made in September 1958, when at that year's Farnborough Show Okanagan Helicopters of Vancouver, Canada, announced an order for one Rotodyne.

Other potential buyers, from the USA and Japan, were also being slowly reeled in, but continued British Government financial support depended on a BEA order, which was still not forthcoming. Apart from performance shortcomings, BEA was concerned by the shattering noise generated by the Rotodyne, and the airline's tentative announcement in January 1959 that it would order six hinged on radical improvements in the developed aircraft.

In 1960 the aircraft and

helicopter activities of Fairey Aviation and Westland Aircraft were merged, and the announcement of an injection of £4 million of Government money made the project look reasonably secure. But then, in April 1960, Okanagan pulled out, disturbed at the lack of progress. New York Airways followed in September, and as the project lost momentum it was soon clear that Government funds would soon be cut off. Cancellation finally came in February 1962.

Handley Page (Reading) HPR 3 Herald G-AODE in Queensland Airlines livery

Handley Page Herald

As originally conceived in the early 1950s the Herald was a four-engined enlargement of the Marathon with accommodation for 44 passengers. Two prototypes, powered by Leonides Major piston engines and registered G-AODE and 'ODF, were laid down. The first of these made its maiden flight on August 25, 1955, by which time the manufacturer had received orders for a substantial number of aircraft from, amongst others, Queensland Airlines, Australian National Airlines and Lloyd Aero

Colombiano. Production was about to proceed when, in May 1957, it was decided to change to turboprop power in the light of the success being enjoyed by the Viscount and Fokker Friendship. Re-engined with a pair of Rolls-Royce Darts, 'ODE made its first flight in March 1958.

The first Dart Herald order was for three aircraft, placed in June 1959 by the Ministry of Aviation on behalf of BEA's Highlands service. These three Series 100 aircraft, G-APWB, 'PWC and

'PWD, were sold to Autair in 1966. Production of the Series 200 totalled 36, operators including Jersey Airlines, which acquired the first six of these slightly stretched 56-seat aircraft, Air Manila, Eastern Provincial in Canada, Israel Inland Airways and Bavaria Flug. Heralds were still in service in the mid-1970s, operating with British Island Airways, British Midland Airways, Transbrasil, Far Eastern Air Transport, Eastern Provincial and a number of others.

HPR 7 Dart Herald G-ARTC was originally HPR 3 Herald G-AODF

G-AODE after conversion to Dart Herald standard in March 1958

Westland Widgeon

The Westland S-51 Series 2 Widgeon was, as the designation suggests, a developed version of the S-51 Dragonfly with an entirely new forward fuselage seating five people. Powerplant was the 520 hp Alvis Leonides 521/2 and the Widgeon embodied the same rotor head as the S-55 Whirlwind. The prototype, G-ALIK, flew for the first time on August 23, 1955, and was followed by 14 production aircraft, some of which were conversions of existing S-51 Mk 1As. Of the 14, two were for the Brazilian Navy, one for the Royal Arab Air Force, one for Japan and the rest were registered in Britain. UK helicopter operator Bristow used seven Widgeons at one time or another.

Westland S-51 Mk 1A G-AKTW before conversion

Cheetah-engined Lancashire Prospector Series 2 G-ARDG

Edgar Percival EP.9

Australian pilot and engineer Edgar Percival founded the original Percival Company in 1932 and was responsible for the well known Percival Gull series of light aircraft. He re-entered the British aircraft industry with the private-venture single-engined EP.9 utility aircraft, the prototype of which was built at Stapleford Tawney in Essex. First flight of G-AOFU was made by the designer on December 21, 1955.

A total of 21 EP.9s were built, 13 of which were initially registered in Britain. Two were evaluated by the British Army and were delivered to Middle Wallop wearing military serials; they returned to the UK register in 1962. Civil operators were many and varied, and EP.9s were to be found in Europe, Australia and New Zealand as well as Britain.

In 1958 Percival sold his majority shareholding in Edgar Percival Ltd, together with design rights to the EP.9, to Samlesbury Engineering Ltd. The latter company changed its name to Lancashire Aircraft Co Ltd and proceeded with construction of a modified version of the EP.9, powered by a 295 hp Lycoming engine driving a three-bladed propeller, known as the Lancashire Aircraft Prospector.

G-AKTW after conversion to Series 2 Widgeon standard in 1955

Edgar Percival EP.9 G-AOFU

Trans-Canada Airlines Vanguard at Farnborough

Vickers Vanguard and Merchantman

The Vanguard was a BEA-inspired Viscount replacement which did not quite come off. The original Type 900 concept called for a Tyne-engined aircraft with a capacity of 93 passengers or a payload of 21,000lb. This was felt to be on the small side and Vickers accordingly scaled up the design to produce the 126-passenger Type 950 Vanguard.

Construction of the prototype began in 1956 and in July of that year BEA concluded an agreement for the purchase of 20 aircraft to be designated Type 951. In January 1957 Vickers secured an order for 20 (later increased to 23) of an improved and heavier version, the Type 952, for Trans Canada Airlines. BEA then realised that the heavier aircraft more closely matched its operational philosophy and amended its order to six 951s (already in production at that time) and fourteen 953s of the same weight as the Canadian aircraft.

First flight of the prototype, G-AOYW, took place from Brooklands on January 20, 1959, followed on April 22 by the first flight of 'PEA, first of BEA's Type 951s. Scheduled flights in TCA service began in February 1961, with the first of the British airline's scheduled European flights taking place at the beginning of the following month. First freighter conversion was carried out by the renamed Air Canada in 1966, the aircraft being known as the Cargoliner. In its new form it could carry up to 42,000lb of freight and was successful enough to prompt BEA to follow Air Canada's line, converting nine Vanguards to Merchantmen from 1969.

Air Canada had disposed of all of its Vanguards by the end of 1973, 11 being registered in Britain (although several of these were later re-sold abroad). The largest single UK operator was Invicta, which owned seven between October 1970 and November 1975.

Vickers Type 951 Vanguard G-APEB of BEA

Armstrong Whitworth Argosy 101 G-AZHN of Sagittair

Armstrong Whitworth Argosy

The Argosy, last aircraft to carry the Armstrong Whitworth name, originated in the company's reply to Air Ministry requirement OR 323 for a medium-range freight-carrying aircraft able to lift up to 25,000lb. The original studies, carried out in 1955, envisaged a high-wing twin-engined aircraft with twin vertical tails mounted on booms closely set either side of a truncated fuselage with rear loading ramp. This study, the AW 66, was paralleled by a civil version, the AW 65, which was to have full-section doors at either end.

By September 1956, with no prospect of a military order in sight, the company concentrated on the civil design, which crystallised as the AW 650 Argosy.

With some commercial interest being shown, the company laid down an initial batch of ten aircraft plus two structural test airframes. The prototype, G-AOZZ, flew for the first time on January 8, 1959, and the first five Series 102 production aircraft all flew by the end of the year. First order came from

American operator Riddle Airlines of Miami, Fla, which ordered four (later increased to seven) in February 1959; all had been delivered by August 1961. These aircraft subsequently passed into the hands of Calhoun Equipment (renamed Universal Airlines in 1968). Still later, in 1970, four returned to Britain and, after resparring, were acquired by freight carrier Sagittair.

BEA's involvement with the Argosy began with an order for three Series 102 aircraft,

G-AOZZ, 'PRM and 'PRN, all of which had been delivered by December 1961. During 1962 work had started on a new version, the Series 220, with a larger freight hold and uprated Rolls-Royce Dart engines. The first of these, G-ASKZ, flew for the first time on March 11, 1964, and in September BEA placed an order for five, to be known as the Series 222, in part exchange for its old Series 102s. The 222s remained in consistently profitable service with BEA from February 1965 until their eventual withdrawal in April 1970.

OTRAG Range Air Services Argosy 9Q-COA at Hurn in February 1977

BAe 748

Many maufacturers have tried to build a proper DC-3 replacement over the last 30 years and none has really succeeded. Avro (later part of Hawker Siddeley and now British Aerospace) made a brave attempt with its 748, which has sold more than 300 in both civil and military versions since production began in 1961.

Work started on four prototypes in January 1960 and the first of these, G-APZV, flew for the first time at Woodford on June 24 of that year, powered by two Rolls-Royce Dart turboprops. A much needed boost to the project had been provided by the licence agreement signed in July 1959 between Avro and the Indian Government, which wanted to assemble 748s from British components at Kanpur; the first Hindustan Aircraft-assembled aircraft flew on November 1, 1961. Meanwhile, on August 31, 1961, the first of three Series 1 production aircraft for Skyways, G-ARMV, had flown for the first time at Woodford. Total production of the Series 1 ran to 20 aircraft, including 12 for Aerolineas Argentinas.

The Series 2 was a developed version with uprated Dart turboprops. The first of these, the re-engined second prototype Avro 748, G-ARAY, first flew in its new form in November 1961. The first production Series 2 flew in August 1962. Apart from numerous sales to military customers, the 748 has been bought by a large number of airlines, including one or two major carriers such as Brazil's Varig and Indian Airlines.

The Series 2A, which superseded the Series 2 in production from mid-1967, differed only in having yet more powerful Rolls-Royce Dart RDa.7 Mk 534 engines. From early 1979 the 2A was itself superseded by the Series 2B with improved hot-and-high performance. At the time of writing orders for more than 330 have been received, this figure including a number of Andovers for the RAF and no fewer than 79 Indian-assembled aircraft.

BAe 748 Series 101 G-ARMW of Dan-Air Skyways

BAe 748MF Andover G-ARRV

Rousseau Aviation BAe 748 F-BSRA

Aviation Traders ATL 98 Carvair

In 1959, keenly aware of the need for a larger replacement for the Bristol Freighter, A. C. Leftley, chief designer of Aviation Traders Ltd, proposed the conversion of an existing airframe. The basic requirement was for a four-engined aircraft capable of carrying five cars and 25 passengers, and Aviation Traders' choice fell on the Douglas DC-4, which at that time was cheap and plentiful. The old nose was replaced with a bulbous unit containing a hydraulically operated sideways-opening door and an elevated flight deck. Apart from some increase in the height and area of the fin and rudder, the rest of the airframe remained unchanged.

The first converted Carvair was G-ANYB, an ex-World Airways and Air Charter C-54B, which flew for the first time in its new guise on June 21, 1961. Named *Golden Gate Bridge*, it entered service with British United Air Ferries in the following March on vehicle ferry routes to the Continent.

A total of 21 conversions were completed between 1961 and 1968. Other operators, apart from BUAF (later British Air Ferries) with eleven, were Intercontinental and Interocean with one each, Aer Lingus with three, Aviaco with two and Ansett-ANA with three. Five were still in service with BAF in 1976.

The first Carvair

Beagle B.206 Series 1 G-ATHO

British United Air Ferries Carvair

Beagle 206

Beagle Aircraft Ltd, formed in 1962 as a subsidiary of British Executive and General Aviation Ltd, combined the interests of Beagle-Auster Ltd and Beagle-Miles Aircraft Ltd. The former Miles facility at Shoreham was responsible for the design and production of the Beagle 206 twin-engined light transport. Drawing-office work began in November 1960 and the pro-

totype B.206X, G-ARRM, was flown for the first time on August 15, 1961, powered by a pair of 260 hp Rolls-Royce Continental flat-six engines. The second aircraft to fly, B.206Y G-ARXM, was a larger aircraft fitted out as a seven-seater. The first production Series 1 aircraft, G-ASMK, flew for the first time in July 1964. This aircraft was later converted to Series 2 stan-

dard, with more powerful 340 hp Continental engines and an extra rear window.

First civil sales, accounting for three of the eleven Series 1 aircraft built, were to Rolls-Royce Ltd, Maidenhead Organ Studios and Imperial Tobacco Co. Production of the improved Series 2 was slightly healthier at 47 aircraft, 28 of which were registered in Britain. Of these, no

fewer than 18 were re-registered abroad to a wide variety of customers which included the Australian Flying Doctor Service.

Three examples of a ten-seat version, the Series 3, were built; G-AXPV was converted from a standard Series 2, one was unregistered and the third was placed on the British register as G-AWLM.

Beagle B.206 Series 2 G-ATTL

BAC VC10 and Super VC10

This attractive aircraft was produced for operation on BOAC's long-distance routes to Africa and the Far East. Although sold in only modest quantities, the VC10 was one of the best transport aircraft ever produced in Britain. A contract for 35 aircraft was placed by BOAC in January 1958 and construction began at Brooklands exactly a year later. The prototype VC10 Type 1100, G-ARTA, flew for the first time on June 29, 1962, powered by four 21,000lb-thrust Rolls-Royce Conway RCo.42 turbofans.

In 1961 Vickers announced the stretched Super VC10 and BOAC cut back its order for the standard Type 1101 to 12 aircraft and ordered a further 30 of the larger Type 1151s. Services to Lagos with the standard aircraft began in April 1964 and the first Super VC10 service, to New York, took place on April 1, 1965. For a variety of reasons the order for Super VC10s had to be cut back to 17 aircraft, with deliveries spread over several years.

Other VC10s built included two Type 1102s for Ghana Airways, three Type 1103s for British United Airways and one Type 1109 for Laker Airways; all were fitted with a large cargo door on the port side of the forward fuselage and had wing roots of slightly greater chord. East African Airways operated five Type 1154s. Although the total customer list is dismally small, the number of actual operators was somewhat greater as a result of inter-airline leasing. BOAC aircraft were used by Nigeria Airways and Air Ceylon.

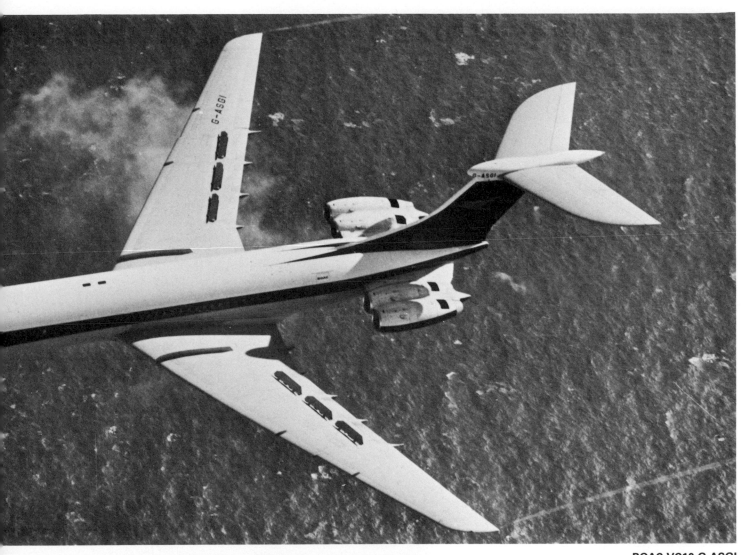

BOAC VC10 G-ASGI

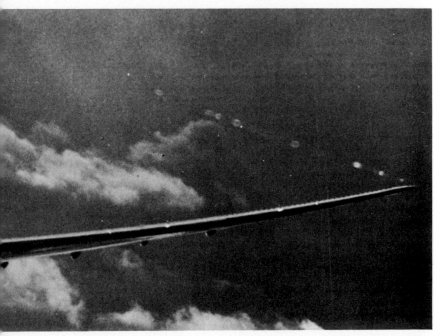

Hawker Siddeley Trident

In 1956 BEA acknowledged that although the basis of its fleet for some years ahead would continue to be the turboprop aircraft, it needed a pure-jet short-haul aircraft to compete with aircraft such as the French Caravelle. In 1957 the airline issued a specification for an 80-seater with a range of up to 1,000 miles, to be in service by 1964. The design submitted by de Havilland was the D.H.121, to be powered by three Rolls-Royce RB.140-141 bypass engines. This was chosen by BEA in February 1958, the airline issuing a letter of intent for the purchase of 24. The D.H.121 was to have a take-off weight of some 131,000lb and to carry up to 111 passengers over stage lengths of 260 to 865 miles. The company's market research department estimated total sales of up to 550 aircraft by 1965.

But in March 1959 BEA sabotaged the highly competitive D.H.121 by announcing that the aircraft was too large and should be scaled down. Inexplicably, the manufacturer submitted and the emasculated HS.121 Trident, powered by three 9,850lb-thrust Rolls-Royce Speys and seating 101 passengers, was the result. The first BEA Trident 1, G-ARPA, flew for the first time on January 9, 1962, and entered service on the airline's European routes on April 1, 1964.

Attempts to increase payload and performance resulted in the introduction of a number of Trident variants over the years. The first improved type was the Trident 1E, seating 115 passengers and powered by three 11,400lb-thrust Spey 511-5s. The first flew for the first time in November 1964, and fifteen were built for delivery to Kuwait Airways, Pakistan International Airlines, Air Ceylon, BKS, Channel Airways and Iraqi Airways.

BEA's improved Trident 1F emerged as the longer-span Trident 2E with increased range, and the airline ordered 15 in August 1965. Furnished to carry 97 tourist-class passengers, the 2E could fly non-stop from London to Beirut and entered service in April 1968. Orders were subsequently received from Cyprus Airways, for two, and from the Chinese airline CAAC, for 33, the last of which was flown on April 17, 1978.

Final version was the 3B, 26 of which were built for British Airways (ex-BEA) from 1969; the first 3B entered service in April 1971. This high-capacity variant can accommodate 128-180 passengers in a lengthened fuselage and has a Rolls-Royce RB.162 boost engine in the tail for improved take-off performance. Two Super Trident 3Bs were also built for the Civil Aviation Administration of China and delivered in 1975. Externally identical to British 3Bs, the Chinese aircraft can accommodate up to 152 passengers and have increased range.

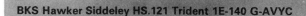

BKS Hawker Siddeley HS.121 Trident 1E-140 G-AVYC

BEA Trident 3 at Helsinki

Trident 1E of Iraqi Airways

Trident 3B-104 G-BAJM before delivery to Chinese flag carrier CAAC

British Aerospace BAe 125 D-COMA

BAe 125

The BAe 125 executive jet began as a design study by de Havilland designer J. Goodwin in 1961. Known briefly as the Jet Dragon, the twin Viper-powered aircraft is produced at Chester, although prototype construction took place at Hatfield. Maiden flight of the first prototype, G-ARYA, took place on August 13, 1962, and this aircraft, together with the second prototype, G-ARYB, was joined by the first production 125, 'RYC, for an intensive certification programme.

Only eight Series 1s were built, this total including the two prototypes, with deliveries to customers beginning in September 1964. Production of the American FAA-certificated Series 1A ran to 64 aircraft, followed by 13 Series 1Bs. This attractive aircraft has continued to sell well, partly on its merits

but also because the manufacturer has learned to employ proper marketing techniques, particularly in the United States, where competition from the home industry is fierce.

Two Series 3 crew trainers were specially built for Qantas in 1965, these aircraft preceding 12 Series 3As for North America, 15 3Bs for the rest of the world, and 36 3A-RA and 3B-RA aircraft with increased all-up weight and fuel capacity. The luxuriously appointed Series 400A and 400B were announced in September 1968, with seating for up to seven and all-up weight increased to 23,000lb; production of these two versions amounted to 116.

The Series 600, a larger, faster development offering 20 per cent more payload and designed for the American market, was announced in 1971. The

lengthened fuselage could accommodate up to 14 passengers and other changes included strengthened wings with modified control surfaces, deletion of the cockpit canopy fairing, and provision of an additional fuel tank in an extended dorsal fin. Production of this variant amounted to 72 aircraft.

Current production version is the Series 700, introduced in 1976. Powered by two 3,700lb-thrust Garrett-AiResearch TFE731 turbofans, the new aircraft also incorporates a number of detail design changes which contribute to both its appearance and performance. By the late summer of 1978 some 52 had been ordered, several by North American customers. As in the Series 600, accommodation is available for either eight in executive layout or 14 in high-density configuration.

BAe 125 Series 600B G-BCUX in July 1975

BAe 125 Series 700A G-BFAN

Shorts Skyvan of Olympic Airways

Skyvan of Gulf Air

Shorts Skyvan

The origins of this most unsophisticated of commercial aircraft lie in George Miles' "one-ton truck," the Aerovan. After Miles Aircraft Ltd folded in 1948, Aerovan service support was concentrated at Shoreham with F. G. Miles Ltd, which converted one well used example to incorporate a special high-aspect-ratio wing designed by Avions Hurel-Dubois of Villacoublay, France. This weird hybrid was known as the Miles HDM 105 and flew at Shoreham between March 1957 and June 1958. Registered G-AHDM, it was the forerunner of the projected HDM 106 Caravan. The HDM 106 was not put into production but the design was sold to Short Brothers, which established a Light Aircraft Division at Belfast in April 1959. The basic HDM 106 idea was substantially reworked by Shorts and emerged as the boxy SC-7, afterwards called the Skyvan.

Construction of the prototype, G-ASCN, began in 1960 but the first flight did not take place until January 17, 1963, the aircraft powered by two 390 hp Continental GTSIO-520 piston engines. Later that year it was re-engined with a pair of 520 hp Astazou II turboprops. Authorisation for a production batch of 20 Skyvans was given in February 1964 and a further batch of 30 was laid down in April 1966. Production aircraft were powered by 730 hp Astazou XIIs, but early in 1967 it was announced that Series 2 aircraft with these engines could not meet performance specifications under hot-and-high conditions and an alternative powerplant was sought. Successful contender was the Garrett AiResearch TPE331 and aircraft thus equipped were designated Series 3s; a number of Series 2s have also been retrospectively modified.

Current production versions include the Series 3 and the Skyliner, an all-passenger version accommodating 22 people plus crew.

Skyvan of Gulf Air

BAe One-Eleven

The origins of the BAe One-Eleven lie in the 32-seat Hunting H.107 of 1956, which was originally to have been powered by a pair of Bristol Orpheus 12Bs. Later the powerplant was changed to the Bristol Siddeley BS.75 turbofan, but the project did not gather momentum until Hunting's absorption into the British Aircraft Corporation in 1960. It was then reworked, emerging first as the BAC 107 and later as the definitive BAC One-Eleven, powered by Rolls-Royce Speys and seating up to 69 passengers.

British United Airways ordered ten Series 200s, with options on a further five. With its second order, six aircraft for Braniff International Airways, the aircraft broke into the North American market.

The Series 200 prototype flew for the first time at Hurn on August 20, 1963, but crashed in Wiltshire in October that year after failing to recover from a deep stall. First commercial services were flown by BUA on April 9, 1965, and by Braniff just a few days later. Later that year the roll of users was expanded to include Aer Lingus and Mohawk.

The prototype Series 300/400 was first flown in July 1965, powered by the more powerful 11,400lb-thrust Spey 511 and having increased payload. The Series 400 was equipped specifically for the American market with such additional equipment as lift-dumpers and drop-out oxygen system; FAA type approval was given in late November 1965. A further development of the Series 300/400 was the Series 500, which incorporated a lengthened fuselage with accommodation for 97-119 passengers. Other improvements included increased wing area and uprated Spey 512 engines. The prototype, which was the converted Series 400 development aircraft G-ASYD, flew for the first time in June 1967; the first production aircraft, G-AVMH, was ARB certificated the following year. Two years later BAC announced the Series 475, which combined the standard fuselage of the Series 300/400 with the longer-span wings of the Series 500.

Latest version of this versatile airliner is the Series 670, an adaptation of the Series 475 which is designed to serve as a replacement for the NAMC YS-11 in Japan.

Total One-Eleven sales had reached more than 220 by April 1978.

BAe One-Eleven EC-BQF of Spanish carrier TAE

One-Eleven 475 G-ASYD with hush-kitted Speys

One-Eleven 432FD G-AXMU of British Island Airways

One-Eleven 518EG G-AXMH of the now
defunct Court Line

Britten-Norman Islander

BN-2A-3 Islander

The Britten-Norman Islander can almost claim the distinction of being a true Dragon Rapide replacement for cheap feeder-liner and charter operations. The prototype, G-ATCT, flew for the first time on June 13, 1965, powered by a pair of Rolls-Royce Continental IO-360 engines. These engines were later changed for more powerful 260 hp Lycoming O-540s and production aircraft also had a wing of slightly increased span. With its boxy fuselage and fixed undercarriage the Islander lacked the grace of the fleet American twins, but with an initial price tag of less than £20,000 it was bound to attract commercial interest.

The production prototype, G-ATWU, flew for the first time on August 20, 1966, in the livery of Scottish carrier Loganair. A British certificate of airworthiness was awarded in August 1967 and the all-important US FAA certificate was granted in the following December. Islander production has since reached the creditable figure of more than 800 machines, although a good number of these are military or paramilitary aircraft.

Main production versions of the civil aircraft are the BN-2A and the current aircraft, the BN-2B Islander II, which differs from earlier variant in having a higher maximum landing weight and improved interior fittings.

Scottish Aviation Jetstream

The H.P.137 Jetstream was a vain attempt by a British aircraft manufacturer to break into the executive/feederliner market, traditionally dominated by American manufacturers like Beech and Cessna. It was also the last design to be initiated by the venerable Handley Page company.

Detailed design work began in late 1965 and the project was announced publicly in January 1966 when the Board of Handley Page authorised manufacture of four prototypes. The semi-monocoque pressurised fuselage was designed to accommodate up to 18 passengers in some comfort, and the specified two 840 ehp Turboméca Astazou turboprops would give the aircraft a cruising speed of around 250 mph at altitude. A production line was established at Radlett to build up to 500 Jetstreams, and at the 1966 Farnborough Show HP announced

receipt of options on 65 aircraft in the USA, where K. R. Cravens' Riley Jetstream Corporation was to handle sales and servicing. In Britain CSE Aviation was appointed distributor and service agent for Europe, Asia and Africa.

First aircraft to fly was G-ATXH, on August 18, 1967, temporarily powered by a pair of 690 ehp Astazou 12s. The definitive engines were fitted in November. Although some delays had begun to accumulate, US Defence Secretary Robert McNamara and Air Force Secretary Harold Brown ordered a trial batch of 11 Jetstreams in response to the US Air Force's CX requirement for a light twin-turboprop mission-support transport. These aircraft were to be powered by Garrett-AiResearch TPE331s and to have an all-up weight of 14,500lb.

By the time that the first production aircraft started flying, in

late 1968, the company had spent some £5½ million on development. The production programme was originally to have been ten batches of 50 aircraft at a rate of 15 per month, but the expected orders were not forthcoming and both the programme and the company began to slide faster and faster towards disaster. Despite its lack of success in Britain the Jetstream did achieve some modest initial sales in the US, with Cal-State Air Lines of Long Beach, California, boasting the largest individual fleet in that country.

By mid-August 1969, however, Handley Page had gone into voluntary liquidation. Despite an eleventh-hour attempt by Cravens Corporation to rescue the company and protect its Jetstream investment, the company was wound up at the end of February 1970. This was not the end of the Jet-

stream, however. Capt Bill Bright of Terravia Trading, together with Scottish Aviation, a significant sub-contractor in past Jetstream manufacture, formed Jetstream Aircraft Ltd and put into effect plans to complete some 20 airframes. The acquisition by Scottish Aviation of all Jetstream production and design rights, together with all jigs, components and aircraft in progress, coincided with the announcement of a Ministry of Defence order for 25 aircraft for the RAF. The first of these Series 200 aircraft was flown in April 1973.

At the end of 1978 there were some 30 civil Jetstreams still in service. Scottish Aviation — now renamed British Aerospace, Scottish Division — was assessing the merits of an improved civil version, provisionally designated Jetstream 31 and intended to meet the requirements of FAR Part 25.

Scottish Aviation Jetstream 1 G-AWVK, operated by Decca

Jetstream F-BTMI of Air Wasteels

BAe/Aérospatiale Concorde

Concorde is the West's first — and to date only — supersonic commercial airliner and there are good grounds to suppose that it will remain unique for at least a further decade or two. Produced jointly by Britain and France, this highly distinctive aircraft originated in the late 1950s in a series of European studies directed at producing a supersonic airliner design which would be competitive with proposed US projects.

In 1959 the British Government's Supersonic Transport Advisory Committee (STAC) recommended two concepts: a Mach 1.2 medium-range design

and a Mach 1.8 long-range model. Meanwhile, the French Government, working in collaboration with Air France, identified a similar requirement. Dassault, Sud Aviation and Nord were each invited to submit designs, and the Sud proposal was selected for further development in mid-1961. At this stage an initial in-service date of 1968 was set, together with an estimated unit cost of about £15 million, excluding production tooling costs.

Following a year of negotiations a consortium agreement was signed by the British and French governments in

November 1962. BAC (as the former Bristol Aeroplane Company had by then been named) and Sud Aviation (later Aérospatiale) had already signed their own agreements, as had engine contractors Bristol Siddeley and Snecma.

The first prototype was rolled out at Toulouse in December 1967, flew for the first time in March 1969, and reached its maximum design cruising speed of Mach 2 in August 1970. The first British prototype was rolled out at Filton in April 1969. After an extensive flight-test programme, the longest ever required for a civil airliner, Con-

corde entered service simultaneously with British Airways and Air France in January 1976, operating initially between London and Bahrain with British Airways, and Paris and Rio de Janeiro (via Dakar) with Air France.

After protracted negotiations and legal battles the two airlines were in 1976 finally allowed to operate services from London and Paris to the US, the role for which the aircraft had originally been designed. But the rising cost of fuel and the increase in low-cost air travel made possible by the new generation of wide-bodied aircraft had made

BAe/Aérospatiale Concorde G-BOAA

Concorde 01 G-AXON at Duxford museum

Concorde less attractive and the options held by the major airlines had been allowed to lapse. Until recently options on three aircraft were held by Iran Air, but these were cancelled following the change in government in that country. The upheaval in Iran also caused another increase in fuel prices and British Caledonian dropped its plans to operate one of the unsold aircraft on its South American routes.

At present Concorde operates between London, New York, Washington and Bahrain with British Airways, and between Paris, New York, Washington and Rio with Air France. In addition, interline agreements between the two airlines and Braniff International allow the latter's crews to operate the aircraft between Washington and Dallas/Fort Worth. A similar agreement between British Airways and Singapore International Airlines allows SIA crews to operate the airaft between Bahrain and Singapore.

In mid-1979 the British and French governments began winding up their financial involvement in the project and announced that no further development of supersonic transport aircraft would be supported. At the time of the announcement a total of 16 production aircraft had been built. Of these, five are in service with British Airways, four with Air France and five remain unsold. Unless the Chinese carrier CAAC exercises its options on three aircraft it is possible that at least some of the unsold aircraft will be transferred to the present carriers at a later date; two prototype and two pre-production aircraft are preserved in British and French museums.

Concorde has been continually attacked by environmental groups. These organisations are still greatly concerned about the high-flying Concorde's effect on the ozone layer in the atmosphere, even though the SST was cleared by tests conducted during the US Climatic Impact Assessment programme in 1973. The aircraft has also attracted more deserved criticism for its shattering noise levels, the nuisance being worst in the region of the international airports from which it operates. Unquestionably a technological *tour de force*, Concorde has proved to be a commercial and environmental failure.

Above and below: Concorde G-BSST

Britten-Norman Trislander

The enlargement of the basic Islander airframe to cater for operators who wanted more seats at minimum cost was logical and inevitable; the way in which Britten-Norman achieved it was quite unorthodox. On both engineering and economic grounds, neither an enlarged twin-engined layout nor a new four-engined airframe appealed to Britten-Norman, and accordingly a third, tail-mounted engine was proposed. Probably unique, this arrangement allowed the manufacturer to keep the Islander's basic 260 hp engines, while the 50 per cent increase in power almost exactly matched the increase in gross weight.

First flight was made on September 11, 1970, with the aircraft, G-ATWU, making an unscheduled appearance at that year's Farnborough Show. By the end of that year three production aircraft were being built by taking standard Islander airframes and inserting a new 7ft 6in section forward of the wing.

ARB certification was granted on May 14, 1971, and the first production aircraft, G-AYTU, was delivered to Aurigny Air Services in the Channel Islands on June 29. However, production plans were interrupted by the manufacturer's bankruptcy in late 1971, caused by the withdrawal of the financial support of Lloyds Bank subsidiary Exporters Finance Corporation. Acquired by the Fairey Company in August 1972, Britten-Norman continued to build Trislanders, but at a very slow rate. Over the next two years production was gradually transferred to Fairey's Belgian subsidiary at Gosselies, which was turning out three Trislanders a month by the end of 1976. In October 1977 the Fairey Group collapsed and Britten-Norman had yet another owner by July 1978, when Pilatus of Switzerland acquired all of the assets of Britten-Norman (Bembridge) Ltd. By the middle of 1978 orders had been received for more than 80 Trislanders, of which some 60 had been delivered to customers in the UK, Africa, Australasia, USA, Canada, Indonesia and South America.

Britten-Norman BN-2A Mk III Trislander G-AYTU before delivery to Aurigny Air Services

Trislander of JFA over Cranfield

Shorts 330 G-BGNA of Scottish carrier Loganair

Shorts 330

The 30-passenger Shorts 330, originally designated SD3-30, is designed primarily for commuter work and is a logical development of the smaller Skyvan.

Preliminary design work started early in 1973, with the first flight scheduled for mid-1974. Despite an extremely tight schedule and the three-day week which afflicted British industry the manufacturer suc-

ceeded in getting prototype G-BSBH airborne for the first time on August 22, 1974. The second aircraft took longer to complete, mainly because it was to be finished to production standard, and it did not fly until the following July. CAA certification followed in January 1976.

From the outset it seemed certain that the structurally simple 330 would be commercially suc-

cessful. First orders for the aircraft came from Command Airways of Poughkeepsie, New York, which had ordered three aircraft only eight days before the first flight. Command is a typical third-level operator, flying services into New York's Kennedy and La Guardia airports from surrounding cities and points such as Boston, Burlington and White Plains. The second operator to place an

order was the Canadian carrier Time Air of Lethbridge, Alberta. Initial deliveries began in June 1976, with the first aircraft going to Time Air.

Other orders have since been placed by DLT of Frankfurt, Golden West of California, Henson Aviation of Maryland, ALM of the Dutch Antilles, Hawaiian Air, Suburban Airlines of Pennsylvania and Chautauqua Airlines of New York.

Shorts 330 in Golden West colours

Shorts 330 D-CDLD of Frankfurt-based airline DLT

Type	Powerplant	Dimensions	Weights	Performance	Accommodation
de Havilland D.H.4	One 375 hp Rolls-Royce Eagle VIII	Wing span: 42ft 4⅝in Length: 30ft 6in Height: 11ft 0in Wing area: 434 sq ft	Empty: 2,387lb AUW: 3,472lb	Max speed: 143 mph Endurance: 3¾hr	Crew: 1 Passengers: 1-2
de Havilland D.H.4A	One 375 hp Rolls-Royce Eagle VIII	Wing span: 42ft 4⅝in Length: 30ft 6in Height: 11ft 0in Wing area: 434 sq ft	Empty: 2,600lb AUW: 3,720lb	Max speed: 121 mph	Crew: 1 Passengers: 2
de Havilland D.H.9	One 230 hp BHP or one 240 hp Siddeley Puma	Wing span: 42ft 4⅝in Length: 30ft 6in Height: 11ft 2in Wing area: 434 sq ft	Empty: 2,193lb AUW: 3,420lb	Max speed: 114 mph Endurance: 4hr	Crew: 1 Passengers: 1-2
de Havilland D.H.9A	One 375 hp Rolls-Royce Eagle VIII	Wing span: 45ft 11⅜in Length: 30ft 3in Height: 11ft 4in Wing area: 486 sq ft	Empty: 2,705lb AUW: 4,223lb	Cruising speed: 111 mph Endurance: 3½hr	Crew: 1 Passengers: 1-2
de Havilland D.H.16	One 320 hp Rolls-Royce Eagle VIII or 450 hp Napier Lion	Wing span: 46ft 5⅞in Length: 30ft 3in Height: 11ft 4in Wing area: 489¾ sq ft	Empty: 3,155lb AUW: 4,750lb	Max speed: 136 mph Cruising speed: 100 mph Range: 425 miles	Crew: 1 Passengers: 4
Handley Page O/400	Two 360 hp Rolls-Royce Eagle VIII	Wing span: 100ft 0in Length: 62ft 10in Height: 22ft 0in Wing area: 1,648 sq ft	Empty: 8,326lb AUW: 12,050lb	Max speed: 97 mph Endurance: 7½hr	Crew: 2 Passengers: 14 (O/7) 12 (O/10) 5 (O/11)
BAT FK.26	One 350 hp Rolls-Royce Eagle VIII	Wing span: 46ft 0in Length: 34ft 8in Height: 11ft 3in Wing area: 580 sq ft	AUW: 4,500lb	Max speed: 122 mph Range: 600 miles	Crew: 1 Passengers: 4
Vickers Vimy Commercial	Two 360 hp Rolls-Royce Eagle VIII	Wing span: 67ft 2in Length: 42ft 8in Height: 15ft 7½in Wing area: 1,330 sq ft	Empty: 7,790lb AUW: 12,500lb	Max speed: 98 mph Cruising speed: 84 mph Range: 450 miles	Crew: 2 Passengers: 10
Avro 504M	One 100 hp Gnome Monosoupape	Wing span: 36ft 0in Length: 29ft 5in Height: 10ft 5in Wing area: 330 sq ft	Empty: 1,220lb AUW: 1,975lb	Max speed: 98 mph Cruising speed: 85 mph Endurance: 3hr	Crew: 1 Passengers: 2-3
Blackburn Kangaroo	Two 270 hp Rolls-Royce Falcon III	Wing span (upper): 74ft 10¼in (lower): 53ft 1in Length: 44ft 2in Height: 16ft 10in Wing area: 868 sq ft	Empty: 5,300lb AUW: 8,100lb	Max speed: 98 mph Cruising speed: 86 mph Range: 410 miles	Crew: 1 Passengers: 8
Bristol Type 47 Tourer	One 230 hp Siddeley Puma	Wing span: 39ft 5in Length: 26ft 1in Height: 10ft 0in Wing area: 407 sq ft	Empty: 1,900lb AUW: 3,000lb	Max speed: 120 mph Range: 400 miles	Crew: 1 Passengers: 2
de Havilland D.H.18B	One 450 hp Napier Lion	Wing span: 51ft 2¾in Length: 39ft 0in Height: 13ft 0in Wing area: 621 sq ft	Empty: 4,310lb AUW: 7,116lb	Max speed: 128 mph Cruising speed: 100 mph Range: 400 miles	Crew: 1 Passengers: 8
Martinsyde Type A Mk II	One 300 hp Hispano-Suiza	Wing span: 43ft 4in Length: 29ft 1¼in Height: 10ft 6in Wing area: 512 sq ft	Empty: 1,800lb AUW: 4,600lb	Max speed: 115 mph Cruising speed: 100 mph Endurance: 5 hr	Crew: 1 Passengers: 4
Handley Page W.8	Two 450 hp Napier Lion	Wing span: 75ft 0in Length: 60ft 3in Height: 17ft 0in Wing area: 1,456 sq ft	Empty: 8,000lb AUW: 12,250lb	Max speed: 115 mph Cruising speed: 90 mph Range: 500 miles	Crew: 2 Passengers: 12-14
Handley Page W.8b	Two 350 hp Rolls-Royce Eagle VIII	Wing span: 75ft 0in Length: 60ft 1in Height: 17ft 0in Wing area: 1,456 sq ft	Empty: 7,700lb AUW: 12,000lb	Max speed: 104 mph Cruising speed: 101 mph Range: 500 miles	Crew: 2 Passengers: 12-14

Type	Powerplant	Dimensions	Weights	Performance	Accommodation
Westland Limousine I	One 275 hp Rolls-Royce Falcon III	Wing span: 38ft 2in Length: 27ft 9in Height: 10ft 9in Wing area: 440 sq ft	Empty: 2,183lb AUW: 3,383lb	Max speed: 100 mph Cruising speed: 85 mph Range: 290 miles	Crew: 1 Passengers: 3
Westland Limousine II	One 300 hp Hispano-Suiza	Wing span: 37ft 9in Length: 27ft 9in Height: 10ft 9in Wing area: 440 sq ft	Empty: 2,010lb AUW: 3,800lb	Max speed: 100 mph Cruising speed: 90 mph Range: 400 miles	Crew: 1 Passengers: 3
Westland Limousine III	One 450 hp Napier Lion	Wing span: 54ft 0in Length: 33ft 6in Height: 12ft 6in Wing area: 726 sq ft	Empty: 3,823lb AUW: 5,850lb	Max speed: 118 mph Cruising speed: 90 mph Range: 520 miles	Crew: 1 Passengers: 5
Vickers Viking Mk IV	One 450 hp Napier Lion	Wing span: 50ft 0in Length: 34ft 2in Height: 14ft 0in Wing area: 635 sq ft	Empty: 4,040lb AUW: 5,790lb	Max speed: 113 mph Range: 925 miles	Crew: 2 Passengers: 3
Bristol Type 62 Ten-Seater	One 450 hp Napier Lion	Wing span: 54ft 3in Length: 42ft 0in Height: 11ft 0in Wing area: 685 sq ft	Empty: 3,900lb AUW: 6,800lb	Max speed: 122 mph Cruising speed: 118 mph Endurance: 5½hr	Crew: 2 Passengers: 8
Bristol Type 75 Ten-Seater	One 425 hp Bristol Jupiter IV	Wing span: 56ft 0in Length: 40ft 6in Height: 11ft 0in Wing area: 700 sq ft	Empty: 4,000lb AUW: 6,755lb	Max speed: 110 mph Endurance: 5½hr	Crew: 2 Passengers: 8
de Havilland D.H.34	One 450 hp Napier Lion	Wing span: 51ft 4in Length: 39ft 0in Height: 12ft 0in Wing area: 590 sq ft	Empty: 4,574lb AUW: 7,200lb	Max speed: 128 mph Cruising speed: 105 mph Range: 365 miles	Crew: 2 Passengers: 9
Vickers Vulcan Type 61	One 360 hp Rolls-Royce Eagle VIII	Wing span: 49ft 0in Length: 37ft 6in Height: 14ft 3in Wing area: 840 sq ft	Empty: 3,775lb AUW: 6,150lb	Max speed: 105 mph Range: 360 miles	Crew: 1 Passengers: 6-8
Vickers Vulcan Type 74	One 450 hp Napier Lion	Wing span: 49ft 0in Length: 38ft 0in Height: 14ft 3in Wing area: 840 sq ft	Empty: 4,400lb AUW: 6,750lb	Max speed: 112 mph Range 430 miles	Crew: 1 Passengers: 6-8
de Havilland D.H.50	One 230 hp Siddeley Puma	Wing span: 42ft 9in Length: 29ft 9in Height: 11ft 0in Wing area: 434 sq ft	Empty: 2,253lb AUW: 3,900lb	Max speed: 112 mph Cruising speed: 95 mph Range: 380 miles	Crew: 1 Passengers: 3
Vickers Vanguard	Two 650 hp Rolls-Royce Condor	Wing span: 87ft 9in Length: 53ft 10in Height: 17ft 3in Wing area: 2,182 sq ft	Empty: 12,040lb AUW: 18,500lb	Max speed: 112 mph Range: 750 miles	Crew: 2 Passengers: 20
Handley Page W.9 Hampstead	Three 385 hp Armstrong Siddeley Jaguar IV or three 420 hp Bristol Jupiter VI	Wing span: 79ft 0in Length: 60ft 4in Height: 16ft 9in Wing area: 1,563 sq ft	Empty: 8,364lb AUW: 14,500lb	Max speed: 114 mph Cruising speed: 95 mph Range: 400 miles	Crew: 2 Passengers: 14
de Havilland D.H.54 Highclere	One 650 hp Rolls-Royce Condor IIIA	Wing span: 68ft 2in Length: 51ft 0in Height: 15ft 2½in Wing area: 1,004 sq ft	Empty: 6,768lb AUW: 11,250lb	Max speed: 110 mph Cruising speed: 100 mph Range: 400 miles	Crew: 2 Passengers: 12
Handley Page W.10	Two 450 hp Napier Lion or two 480 hp Rolls-Royce F.XI	Wing span: 75ft 0in Length: 58ft 4in Height: 17ft 0in Wing area: 1,456 sq ft	Empty: 8,100lb AUW: 13,780lb	Max speed: 112 mph Range: 500 miles	Crew: 2 Passengers: 16
Armstrong Whitworth Argosy I	Three 385 hp Armstrong Siddeley Jaguar III	Wing span: 90ft 8in Length: 65ft 10in Height: 19ft 10in Wing area: 1,886 sq ft	Empty: 12,000lb AUW: 18,000lb	Max speed: 110 mph Cruising speed: 90 mph Range: 330 miles	Crew: 2 Passengers: 20
Armstrong Whitworth Argosy II	Three 420 hp Armstrong Siddeley Jaguar IVA	Wing span: 90ft 4in Length: 67ft 0in Height: 20ft 0in Wing area: 1,873 sq ft	Empty: 12,090lb AUW: 19,200lb	Max speed: 110 mph Cruising speed: 90 mph Range: 520 miles	Crew: 2 Passengers: 20

Type	Powerplant	Dimensions	Weights	Performance	Accommodation
ANEC III	One 350 hp Rolls-Royce Eagle VIII	Wing span: 60ft 0in Length: 45ft 0in Wing area: 740 sq ft	Empty: 3,470lb AUW: 5,600lb	Max speed: 105 mph Cruising speed: 90 mph	Crew: 1 Passengers: 7-8
Handley Page Hamlet	Three 120 hp Bristol Lucifer IV	Wing span: 52ft 0in Length: 34ft 10in Wing area: 388 sq ft	Empty: 3,105lb AUW: 5,000lb	Max speed: 118 mph Cruising speed: 100 mph	Crew: 2 Passengers: 4-6
de Havilland D.H.66 Hercules	Three 420 hp Bristol Jupiter VI	Wing span: 79ft 6in Length: 55ft 6in Height: 18ft 3in Wing area: 1,547 sq ft	Empty: 9,060lb AUW: 15,660lb	Max speed: 128 mph Cruising speed: 110 mph	Crew: 3 Passengers: 14
de Havilland D.H.61 Giant Moth	One 500 hp Bristol Jupiter XI or one 500 hp Armstrong Siddeley Jaguar or one 525 hp Pratt & Whitney Hornet	Wing span: 52ft 0in Length: 38ft 9in Height: 13ft 1in Wing area: 613 sq ft	Empty: 3,650lb AUW: 7,000lb	Max speed: 132 mph Cruising speed: 110 mph Range: 650 miles	Crew: 1 Passengers: 6
Short Calcutta	Three 540 hp Bristol Jupiter XIF	Wing span: 93ft 0in Length: 66ft 9in Height: 23ft 9in Wing area: 1,825 sq ft	Empty: 13,845lb AUW: 22,500lb	Max speed: 118 mph Cruising speed: 97 mph	Crew: 3 Passengers: 15
de Havilland D.H.75A Hawk Moth	One 240 hp Armstrong Siddeley Lynx VIA	Wing span: 47ft 0in Length: 28ft 10in Height: 9ft 4in Wing area: 334 sq ft	Empty: 2,380lb AUW: 3,650lb	Max speed: 127 mph Cruising speed: 105 mph	Crew: 1 Passengers: 3
Westland Wessex	Three 105 hp Armstrong Siddeley Genet Major or three 140 hp Armstrong Siddeley Genet Major 1A	Wing span: 57ft 6in Length: 38ft 0in Height: 9ft 6in Wing area: 490 sq ft	Empty: 3,891lb AUW: 6,300lb	Max speed: 122 mph Cruising speed: 100 mph Range: 420 miles	Crew: 2 Passengers: 4
Desoutter DAC 1	One 105 hp Cirrus Hermes I or one 115 hp Hermes II	Wing span: 36ft 0in Length: 27ft 0in Height: 7ft 0in Wing area: 190 sq ft	Empty: 1,100lb AUW: 1,900lb	Max speed: 115 mph Cruising speed: 97 mph Range: 400 miles	Crew: 1 Passengers: 2
Saro A.17 Cutty Sark	Two 140 hp Armstrong Siddeley Genet Major I	Wing span: 45ft 0in Length: 34ft 4in Height: 11ft 2in Wing area: 320 sq ft	Empty: 2,725lb AUW: 3,900lb	Max speed: 107 mph Cruising speed: 90 mph Range: 315 miles	Crew: 1 Passengers: 3
Avro 619 Five	Three 105 hp Armstrong Siddeley Genet Major I	Wing span: 47ft 0in Length: 35ft 9in Height: 9ft 6in Wing area: 333 sq ft	Empty: 2,790lb AUW: 4,420lb	Max speed: 118 mph Cruising speed: 95 mph Range: 400 miles	Crew: 1 Passengers: 4
Avro 624 Six	Three 105 hp Armstrong Siddeley Genet Major I	Wing span: 51ft 0in Length: 36ft 0in Height: 9ft 6in Wing area: 360 sq ft	Empty: 3,000lb AUW: 5,000lb	Max speed: 113 mph Cruising speed: 95 mph	Crew: 2 Passengers: 4
Avro 618 Ten	Three 240 hp Armstrong Siddeley Lynx IVC	Wing span: 71ft 3in Length: 47ft 6in Height: 12ft 9in Wing area: 772 sq ft	Empty: 6,020lb AUW: 10,600lb	Max speed: 115 mph Cruising speed: 100 mph Range: 400 miles	Crew: 2 Passengers: 8
Blackburn Segrave	One 120 hp de Havilland Gipsy III	Wing span: 39ft 6in Length: 28ft 6in Height: 7ft 9in Wing area: 230 sq ft	Empty: 2,240lb AUW: 3,300lb	Max speed: 138 mph Cruising speed: 112 mph Range: 450 miles	Crew: 1 Passengers: 5
Handley Page H.P.42	Four 555 hp Bristol Jupiter XFBM (H.P.42W) or 490 hp Bristol Jupiter XIF (H.P.42E)	Wing span: 130ft 0in Length: 89ft 9in Height: 27ft 0in Wing area: 2,989 sq ft	Empty: 17,740lb AUW: 29,500lb (W) 28,000lb (E)	Max speed: 127 mph (W) 120 mph (E) Cruising speed: 100 mph Range: 500 miles	Crew: 4 Passengers: 18-24
Vickers Viastra II	Two 525 hp Bristol Jupiter XIF	Wing span: 70ft 0in Length: 45ft 6in Height: 13ft 6in Wing area: 745 sq ft	Empty: 7,880lb AUW: 10,750lb	Max speed: 145 mph Cruising speed: 128 mph Range: 535 miles	Crew: 2 Passengers: 12
de Havilland D.H.80A Puss Moth	One 120 hp de Havilland Gipsy III or one 130 hp de Havilland Gipsy Major	Wing span: 36ft 9in Length: 25ft 0in Height: 7ft 0in Wing area: 222 sq ft	Empty: 1,265lb AUW: 2,050lb	Max speed: 128 mph Cruising speed: 108 mph Range: 300 miles	Crew: 1 Passengers: 2

Type	Powerplant	Dimensions	Weights	Performance	Accommodation
Spartan Three-Seater II	One 115 hp Cirrus Hermes IIB or one 120 hp Cirrus Hermes IV	Wing span: 28ft 10in Length: 26ft 3in Height: 9ft 8in Wing area: 240 sq ft	Empty: 1,150lb AUW: 1,850lb	Max speed: 107 mph Cruising speed: 95 mph Range: 260 miles	Crew: 1 Passengers: 2
General Aircraft Monospar ST-3	Two 50 hp British Salmson AD.9	Wing span: 38ft 0in Length: 21ft 11½in Height: 9ft 0in Wing area: 183 sq ft	Empty: 1,057lb AUW: 1,800lb	Max speed: 110 mph Cruising speed: 95 mph	Crew: 1 Passengers: 2
General Aircraft Monospar ST-4	Two 85 hp Pobjoy R	Wing span: 40ft 2in Length: 26ft 4in Height: 7ft 0in Wing area: 219 sq ft	Empty: 1,480lb AUW: 2,550lb	Max speed: 130 mph Cruising speed: 115 mph Range: 540 miles	Crew: 1 Passengers: 3-4
General Aircraft Monospar ST-6	Two 85 hp Pobjoy R or two 90 hp Pobjoy Niagara I	Wing span: 40ft 2in Length: 26ft 4in Height: 7ft 0in Wing area: 219 sq ft	Empty: 1,500lb AUW: 2,600lb	Max speed: 135 mph Cruising speed: 120 mph Range: 550 miles	Crew: 1 Passengers: 4-5
General Aircraft Monospar ST-10	Two 90 hp Pobjoy Niagara I	Wing span: 40ft 2in Length: 26ft 4in Height: 7ft 10in Wing area: 217 sq ft	Empty: 1,470lb AUW: 2,750lb	Max speed: 142 mph Cruising speed: 130 mph Range: 585 miles	Crew: 1 Passengers: 4-5
General Aircraft Monospar ST-12	Two 130 hp de Havilland Gipsy Major	Wing span: 40ft 2in Length: 26ft 4in Height: 7ft 10in Wing area: 217 sq ft	Empty: 1,840lb AUW: 2,875lb	Max speed: 158 mph Cruising speed: 142 mph Range: 410 miles	Crew: 1 Passengers: 4-5
Short Kent	Four 555 hp Bristol Jupiter XFBM	Wing span: 113ft 0in Length: 78ft 5in Height: 28ft 0in Wing area: 2,640 sq ft	Empty: 20,460lb AUW: 32,000lb	Max speed: 137 mph Cruising speed: 105 mph Range: 450 miles	Crew: 3 Passengers: 15
Short Valetta	Three 525 hp Bristol Jupiter XIF	Wing span: 107ft 0in Length: 70ft 5in Wing area: 1,382 sq ft	Empty: 14,535lb AUW: 23,000lb	Max speed: 135 mph Cruising speed: 0 Range: 525 miles	Crew: 2 Passengers: 16
Airspeed AS.4 Ferry	One 120 hp de Havilland Gipsy III and two 120 hp de Havilland Gipsy II	Wing span: 55ft 0in Length: 39ft 8in Height: 14ft 3in Wing area: 610 sq ft	Empty: 3,300lb AUW: 5,400lb	Max speed: 112 mph Cruising speed: 100 mph Range: 340 miles	Crew: 1 Passengers: 10
Armstrong Whitworth A.W.15 Atalanta	Four 340 hp Armstrong Siddeley Serval III	Wing span: 90ft 0in Length: 71ft 6in Height: 15ft 0in Wing area: 1,285 sq ft	Empty: 13,940lb AUW: 21,000lb	Max speed: 156 mph Cruising speed: 130 mph Range: 400 miles	Crew: 3 Passengers: 9
Blackburn Biplane	Two 400 hp Armstrong Siddeley Jaguar IVC	Wing span: 64ft 0in Length: 55ft 0in Height: 16ft 0in Wing area: 1,037 sq ft	Empty: 7,931lb AUW: 12,150lb	Max speed: 118 mph Cruising speed: 110 mph Range: 350 miles	Crew: 2 Passengers: 10
Blackburn Monoplane	Two 400 hp Armstrong Siddeley Jaguar IVC	Wing span: 86ft 0in Length: 55ft 3in Height: 16ft 9in Wing area: 1,068 sq ft	Empty: 8,818lb AUW: 13,074lb	Max speed: 128 mph Cruising speed: 110 mph Range: 350 miles	Crew: 2 Passengers: 10
de Havilland D.H.83 Fox Moth	One 130 hp de Havilland Gipsy Major	Wing span: 30ft 10¾in Length: 25ft 9in Height: 8ft 9½in Wing area: 261 sq ft	Empty: 1,100lb AUW: 2,070lb	Max speed: 123 mph Cruising speed: 105 mph Range: 415 miles	Crew: 1 Passengers: 4
Spartan Cruiser II	Three 130 hp de Havilland Gipsy Major or three 130 hp Cirrus Hermes IV or three 130 hp Walter Major 4	Wing span: 54ft 0in Length: 39ft 2in Height: 10ft 0in Wing area: 436 sq ft	Empty: 3,650lb AUW: 6,200lb	Max speed: 133 mph Cruising speed: 115 mph Range: 310 miles	Crew: 2 Passengers: 6
de Havilland D.H.84 Dragon	Two 130 hp de Havilland Gipsy Major I	Wing span: 47ft 4in Length: 34ft 6in Height: 10ft 1in Wing area: 376 sq ft	Empty: 2,300lb AUW: 4,200lb	Max speed: 128 mph Cruising speed: 109 mph Range: 460 miles	Crew: 1 Passengers: 6
Airspeed AS.5 Courier	One 240 hp Armstrong Siddeley Lynx IVC	Wing span: 47ft 0in Length: 28ft 6in Height: 8ft 9in Wing area: 250 sq ft	Empty: 2,344lb AUW: 3,900lb	Max speed: 153 mph Cruising speed: 132 mph Range: 635 miles	Crew: 1 Passengers: 5

Type	Powerplant	Dimensions	Weights	Performance	Accommodation
Short Scion 2	Two 90 hp Pobjoy Niagara III or two 90 hp de Havilland Gipsy Major	Wing span: 42ft 0in Length: 31ft 6in Height: 10ft 4½in Wing area: 255 sq ft	Empty: 1,770lb AUW: 3,200lb	Max speed: 128 mph Cruising speed: 116 mph Range: 390 miles	Crew: 1 Passengers: 15
Boulton and Paul P.64 Mailplane	Two 555 hp Bristol Pegasus I.M.2	Wing span: 54ft 0in Length: 42ft 6in	Empty: 6,125lb AUW: 10,500lb	Cruising speed: 172 mph Range: 1,250 miles	Crew: 2
Boulton and Paul P.71A	Two 490 hp Armstrong Siddeley Jaguar VIA	Wing span: 54ft 0in Length: 44ft 2in	Empty: 6,100lb AUW: 9,500lb	Cruising speed: 150 mph Range: 600 miles	Crew: 2
BA Eagle	One 130 hp de Havilland Gipsy Major	Wing span: 39ft 3in Length: 26ft 0in Height: 6ft 9in Wing area: 200 sq ft	Empty: 1,450lb AUW: 2,400lb	Max speed: 148 mph Cruising speed: 130 mph Range: 650 miles	Crew: 1 Passengers: 2
Vickers Vellox	Two 600 hp Bristol Perseus III	Wing span: 76ft 0in Length: 50ft 6in	Empty: 8,150lb AUW: 13,500lb	Cruising speed: 130 mph Range: 690 miles	Crew: 3 Passengers: 10
Avro 642	Two 450 hp Armstrong Siddeley Jaguar VID	Wing span: 71ft 3in Length: 54ft 6in Height: 11ft 6in Wing area: 728 sq ft	Empty: 7,360lb AUW: 11,800lb	Max speed: 156 mph Cruising speed: 125 mph Range: 600 miles	Crew: 2 Passengers: 16
Airspeed AS.6J Envoy	Two 350 hp Armstrong Siddeley Cheetah IX	Wing span: 52ft 4in Length: 34ft 6in Height: 9ft 6in Wing area: 339 sq ft	Empty: 4,340lb AUW: 6,600lb	Max speed: 203 mph Cruising speed: 170 mph Range: 620 miles	Crew: 1 Passengers: 6-8
de Havilland D.H.86	Four 200 hp de Havilland Gipsy Six Series I	Wing span: 64ft 6in Length: 46ft 1in Height: 13ft 0in Wing area: 641 sq ft	Empty: 6,303lb AUW: 1,000lb	Max speed: 170 mph Cruising speed: 145 mph Range: 760 miles	Crew: 2 Passengers: 10
de Havilland D.H.89 Dragon Rapide	Two 200 hp de Havilland Gipsy Queen 3	Wing span: 48ft 0in Length: 34ft 6in Height: 10ft 3in Wing area: 336 sq ft	Empty: 3,230lb AUW: 5,500lb	Max speed: 157 mph Cruising speed: 132 mph Range: 520 miles	Crew: 2 Passengers: 6
Short L.17 Scylla	Four 595 hp Bristol Jupiter XFBM	Wing span: 113ft 0in Length: 83ft 10in	Empty: 22,650lb AUW: 33,500lb	Cruising speed: 105 mph	Crew: 2 Passengers: 38
Avro 652A Anson 1	Two 350 hp Armstrong Siddeley Cheetah IX	Wing span: 56ft 6in Length: 42ft 3in Height: 9ft 6in Wing area: 410 sq ft	Empty: 5,375lb AUW: 9,540lb	Max speed: 188 mph Cruising speed: 158 mph Range: 660 miles	Crew: 2 Passengers: 6
de Havilland D.H.90 Dragonfly	Two 130 hp de Havilland Gipsy Major	Wing span: 43ft 0in Length: 31ft 8in Height: 9ft 2in Wing area: 256 sq ft	Empty: 2,500lb AUW: 4,000lb	Max speed: 144 mph Cruising speed: 125 mph Range: 625 miles	Crew: 1 Passengers: 4
Heston Phoenix	One 200 hp de Havilland Gipsy VI	Wing span: 40ft 4in Length: 30ft 2in Height: 8ft 7in Wing area: 260 sq ft	Empty: 2,000lb AUW: 3,300lb	Max speed: 145 mph Cruising speed: 135 mph Range: 500 miles	Crew: 1 Passengers: 4
General Aircraft Monospar ST.25 Jubilee	Two 90 hp Pobjoy Niagara II	Wing span: 40ft 2in Length: 26ft 4in Height: 7ft 10in Wing area: 217 sq ft	Empty: 1,680lb AUW: 2,875lb	Max speed: 142 mph Cruising speed: 130 mph Range: 585 miles	Crew: 1 Passengers: 6
Miles M.3A Falcon	One 130 hp de Havilland Gipsy Major	Wing span: 35ft 0in Length: 25ft 0in Height: 6ft 6in Wing area: 174 sq ft	Empty: 1,300lb AUW: 2,200lb	Max speed: 145 mph Cruising speed: 125 mph Range: 615 miles	Crew: 1 Passengers: 3
Short Scion Senior	Four 90 hp Pobjoy Niagara III	Wing span: 55ft 0in Length: 42ft 0in	Empty: 3,886lb (floatplane) 3,546lb (landplane) AUW: 5,750lb (floatplane and landplane)	Max speed: 140 mph (landplane) Cruising speed: 115 mph (floatplane) 122 mph (landplane)	Crew: 1 Passengers: 9
Short S.23 Empire Flying Boat	Four 920 hp Bristol Pegasus XC or four 1,010 hp Bristol Pegasus XXII	Wing span: 114ft 0in Length: 88ft 0in Height: 31ft 9¾in Wing area: 1,500 sq ft	Empty: 23,500lb AUW: 43,500lb	Max speed: 200 mph Cruising speed: 165 mph Range: 760 miles	Crew: 3/4 Passengers: 24

Type	Powerplant	Dimensions	Weights	Performance	Accommodation
de Havilland D.H.91 Albatross	Four 525 hp de Havilland Gipsy Twelve Series I	Wing span: 105ft 0in Length: 71ft 6in Height: 22ft 3in Wing area: 1,078 sq ft	Empty: 21,230lb AUW: 29,500lb	Max speed: 225 mph Cruising speed: 210 mph Range: 1,040 miles	Crew: 4 Passengers: 22
Short-Mayo Composite *Mercury*	Four 340 hp Napier Rapier V	Wing span: 73ft 0in Length: 51ft 0in Wing area: 611 sq ft	Empty: 10,000lb AUW: 15,500lb	Max speed: 207 mph Cruising speed: 180 mph Range: 3,900 miles	Crew: 2
Short-Mayo Composite *Maia*	Four 920 hp Bristol Pegasus XC	Wing span: 114ft 0in Length: 84ft 10¾in Wing area: 1,750 sq ft	Empty: 24,000lb AUW: 38,000lb	Max speed: 200 mph Cruising speed: 165 mph Range: 850 miles	Crew: 3 Passengers: 24
Percival Q6	Two 205 hp de Havilland Gipsy Six Series II	Wing span: 46ft 8in Length: 32ft 3in Height: 9ft 9in Wing area: 278 sq ft	Empty: 3,500lb AUW: 5,500lb	Max speed: 195 mph Cruising speed: 175 mph Range: 750 miles	Crew: 1 Passengers: 5-6
Armstrong Whitworth Ensign 1	Four 850 hp Armstrong Siddeley Tiger IXC	Wing span: 123ft 0in Length: 114ft 0in Height: 23ft 0in Wing area: 2,450 sq ft	Empty: 32,920lb AUW: 49,000lb	Max speed: 205 mph Cruising speed: 170 mph Range: 800 miles	Crew: 5 Passengers: 40
de Havilland D.H.95 Flamingo	Two 890 hp Bristol Perseus XIIC or two 930 hp Bristol Perseus XVI	Wing span: 70ft 0in Length: 51ft 7in Height: 15ft 3in Wing area: 639 sq ft	Empty: 11,325lb AUW: 17,600lb	Max speed: 239 mph Cruising speed: 184 mph Range: 1,210 miles	Crew: 2 Passengers: 12-17
Short S.26 G-class Flying Boat	Four 1,380 hp Bristol Hercules IV or four 1,380 hp Bristol Hercules XIV	Wing span: 134ft 4in Length: 101ft 4in Height: 37ft 7in Wing area: 2,160 sq ft	Empty: 37,700lb AUW: 73,500lb	Max speed: 209 mph Cruising speed: 180 mph Range: 3,200 miles	Crew: 5 Passengers: 40 Cargo: 2 tons
Avro 652A 19 Series 2	Two 420 hp Armstrong Siddeley Cheetah 15	Wing span: 57ft 6in Length: 42ft 3in Height: 13ft 10in Wing area: 440 sq ft	Empty: 6,576lb AUW: 10,400lb	Max speed: 171 mph Cruising speed: 159 mph Range: 660 miles	Crew: 1-2 Passengers: 9
Bristol 170 Freighter Mk IIA	Two 1,675 hp Bristol Hercules 632	Wing span: 98ft 0in Length: 68ft 4in Height: 21ft 8in Wing area: 1,405 sq ft	Empty: 26,910lb AUW: 44,000lb	Max speed: 195 mph Cruising speed: 165 mph Range: 490 miles	Crew: 3 Passengers: 32 Cargo: 4½ tons
Avro Tudor 1	Four 1,770 hp Rolls-Royce Merlin 621	Wing span: 120ft 0in Length: 79ft 6in Height: 20ft 11in Wing area: 1,421 sq ft	Empty: 47,960lb AUW: 71,000lb	Max speed: 260 mph Cruising speed: 210 mph Range: 3,630 miles	Crew: 3 Passengers: 12+
Avro Lancastrian	Four 1,635 hp Rolls-Royce Merlin T.24/4	Wing span: 102ft 0in Length: 76ft 10 in Height: 19ft 6in Wing area: 1,297 sq ft	Empty: 30,426lb AUW: 65,000lb	Max speed: 315 mph Cruising speed: 230 mph Range: 4,150 miles	Crew: 3 Passengers: 9
Avro York	Four 1,620 hp Rolls-Royce Merlin T.24	Wing span: 102ft 0in Length: 78ft 6in Height: 16ft 6in Wing area: 1,205 sq ft	Empty: 42,040lb AUW: 68,000lb	Max speed: 298 mph Cruising speed: 233 mph Range: 2,700 miles	Crew: 3 Passengers: 12
de Havilland D.H.104 Dove	Two 330 hp de Havilland Gipsy Queen 70-3	Wing span: 57ft 0in Length: 39ft 4in Height: 13ft 4in Wing area: 335 sq ft	Empty: 5,650lb AUW: 8,500lb	Max speed: 201 mph Cruising speed: 165 mph Range: 1,000 miles	Crew: 2 Passengers: 8
Handley Page Hermes	Four 2,100 hp Bristol Hercules 763	Wing span: 113ft 0in Length: 96ft 10in Height: 29ft 11in Wing area: 1,408 sq ft	Empty: 55,350lb AUW: 86,000lb	Max speed: 350 mph Cruising speed: 276 mph Range: 2,000 miles	Crew: 7 Passengers: 63
Handley Page Halton	Four 1,675 hp Bristol Hercules 100	Wing span: 103ft 8in Length: 73ft 7in Height: 21ft 7in Wing area: 1,275 sq ft	Empty: 37,830lb AUW: 65,000lb	Max speed: 270 mph Range: 2,050 miles	Crew: 3 Passengers: 10 Cargo: 8,000lb
Miles Gemini	Two 100 hp Blackburn Cirrus Minor 2	Wing span: 36ft 2in Length: 22ft 3in Height: 7ft 6in Wing area: 191 sq ft	Empty: 1,896lb AUW: 3,000lb	Max speed: 140 mph Cruising speed: 125 mph Range: 820 miles	Crew: 1 Passengers: 2-3

Type	Powerplant	Dimensions	Weights	Performance	Accommodation
Miles Aries	Two 155 hp Blackburn Cirrus Major 3	Wing span: 36ft 2in Length: 22ft 3in Height: 7ft 6in Wing area: 191 sq ft	Empty: 2,350lb AUW: 3,475 lb	Max speed: 172 mph Cruising speed: 150 mph Range: 675 miles	Crew: 1 Passengers: 2-3
Vickers Viking 1	Two 1,690 hp Bristol Hercules 634	Wing span: 89ft 3in Length: 62ft 11in Height: 19ft 6in Wing area: 882 sq ft	Empty: 22,910lb AUW: 34,000lb	Max speed: 252 mph Cruising speed: 210 mph Range: 1,875 miles	Crew: 4 Passengers: 21
Miles Aerovan 4	Two 155 hp Blackburn Cirrus Major 3	Wing span: 50ft 0in Length: 36ft 0in Height: 13ft 6in Wing area: 390 sq ft	Empty: 3,000lb AUW: 5,800lb	Max speed: 127 mph Cruising speed: 112 mph Range: 400 miles	Crew: 1-2 Passengers: 6
Short Sunderland 3	Four 1,030 hp Bristol Perseus XVIII	Wing span: 112ft 9½in Length: 88ft 6¾in Height: 22ft 10½in Wing area: 1,687 sq ft	Empty: 35,862lb AUW: 50,000lb	Max speed: 178 mph Cruising speed: 165 mph Range: 2,350 miles	Crew: 3 Passengers: 24 Cargo: 6,500lb
Short Sandringham 7	Four 1,200 hp Pratt & Whitney Twin Wasp R-1830-92D	Wing span: 112ft 9½in Length: 86ft 3in Height: 22ft 10½in Wing area: 1,687 sq ft	Empty: 39,498lb AUW: 60,000lb	Max speed: 206 mph Cruising speed: 176 mph Range: 2,440 miles	Crew: 3 Passengers: 30
Short S.45 Solent 2	Four 1,690 hp Bristol Hercules 637	Wing span: 112ft 9½in Length: 87ft 8in Height: 34ft 3¼in Wing area: 1,687 sq ft	Empty: 47,760lb AUW: 78,000lb	Max speed: 273 mph Cruising speed: 244 mph Range: 1,800 miles	Crew: 3 Passengers: 39
Handley Page Marathon	Four 340 hp de Havilland Gipsy Major 70-3	Wing span: 65ft 0in Length: 52ft 1½in Height: 14ft 1in Wing area: 498 sq ft	Empty: 11,688lb AUW: 18,250lb	Max speed: 232 mph Cruising speed: 201 mph Range: 935 miles	Crew: 2 Passengers: 20
Airspeed AS.65 Consul	Two 395 hp Armstrong Siddeley Cheetah 10	Wing span: 53ft 4in Length: 35ft 4in Height: 11ft 1in Wing area: 348 sq ft	Empty: 6,047lb AUW: 8,250lb	Max speed: 190 mph Cruising speed: 156 mph Range: 900 miles	Crew: 1-2 Passengers: 6
Airspeed AS.57 Ambassador	Two 2,625 hp Bristol Centaurus 661	Wing span: 115ft 0in Length: 82ft 0in Height: 18ft 10in Wing area: 1,200 sq ft	Empty: 35,377lb AUW: 52,500lb	Max speed: 312 mph Cruising speed: 260 mph Range: 550 miles	Crew: 3 Passengers: 28-50
Bristol 171 Sycamore Mk 4	One 550 hp Alvis Leonides LE.214M	Rotor dia: 48ft 7in Length: 42ft 0in Height: 14ft 7in	Empty: 3,810lb AUW: 5,600lb	Max speed: 127 mph Cruising speed: 91 mph Range: 330 miles	Crew: 1 Passengers: 3
Cunliffe-Owen Concordia	Two 550 hp Alvis Leonides LE.4M	Wing span: 56ft 7in Length: 44ft 10in Height: 16ft 8½in Wing area: 435 sq ft	Empty: 4,450lb AUW: 12,500lb	Max speed: 216 mph Cruising speed: 160 mph	Crew: 2 Passengers: 10-14
Percival Prince 3	Two 155 hp Alvis Leonides 502/4	Wing span: 56ft 0in Length: 42ft 10in Height: 16ft 1in Wing area: 365 sq ft	Empty: 8,038lb AUW: 11,000lb	Max speed: 229 mph Cruising speed: 197 mph Range: 894 miles	Crew: 1-2 Passengers: 8
Short Sealand	Two 340 hp de Havilland Gipsy Queen 70-3	Wing span: 61ft 6in Length: 42ft 2in Height: 15ft 0in Wing area: 359 sq ft	Empty: 7,065lb AUW: 9,100lb	Max speed: 185 mph Cruising speed: 169 mph Range: 525 miles	Crew: 2 Passengers: 5-7
Vickers Viscount 720	Four 1,540 ehp Rolls-Royce Dart 506	Wing span: 93ft 8½in Length: 81ft 2in Height: 26ft 9in Wing area: 963 sq ft	Empty: 38,358lb AUW: 64,500lb	Max speed: 380 mph Cruising speed: 316 mph Range: 1,730 miles	Crew: 3 Passengers: 43
Vickers Viscount 810	Four 1,990 ehp Rolls-Royce Dart 525	Wing span: 93ft 8½in Length: 85ft 8in Height: 26ft 9in Wing area: 963 sq ft	Empty: 43,500lb AUW: 72,500lb	Max speed: 357 mph Cruising speed: 320 mph Range: 1,587 miles	Crew: 3 Passengers: 57-65
Armstrong Whitworth Apollo	Four 1,475 ehp Armstrong Siddeley Mamba 504	Wing span: 92ft 0in Length: 71ft 5½in Height: 26ft 0in Wing area: 986 sq ft	Empty: 30,800lb AUW: 45,000lb	Max speed: 330 mph Cruising speed: 276 mph Range: 940 miles	Crew: 2-3 Passengers: 26-31

Type	Powerplant	Dimensions	Weights	Performance	Accommodation
Bristol Brabazon	Eight 2,500 ehp Bristol Centaurus 20	Wing span: 230ft 0in Length: 177ft 0in Height: 50ft 0in Wing area: 5,317 sq ft	Empty: 159,310lb AUW: 290,000lb	Max speed: 300 mph Cruising speed: 250 mph Range: 5,500 miles	Crew: 12 Passengers: 100
de Havilland D.H.106 Comet 1	Four 4,450lb st de Havilland Ghost 50	Wing span: 115ft 0in Length: 93ft 0in Height: 28ft 4in Wing area: 2,015 sq ft	AUW: 105,000lb	Cruising speed: 490 mph at 35,000ft Range: 1,750 miles	Crew: 3-4 Passengers: 36-40
de Havilland D.H.106 Comet 4C	Four 10,500lb st Rolls-Royce Avon 525B	Wing span: 114ft 10in Length: 118ft 0in Height: 28ft 6in Wing area: 2,121 sq ft	AUW: 162,000lb	Cruising speed: 503 mph at 39,000ft Range: 2,650 miles	Crew: 4 Passengers: 72-101
de Havilland D.H.114 Heron	Four 250 hp de Havilland Gipsy Queen 30	Wing span: 71ft 6in Length: 48ft 6in Height: 15ft 7in Wing area: 499 sq ft	Empty: 8,150lb AUW: 13,500lb	Cruising speed: 183 mph Range: 915 miles	Crew: 2 Passengers: 17
Bristol 173	Two 545 hp Alvis Leonides 73	Rotor dia: 48ft 7in Length: 55ft 2in Height: 15ft 0in	Empty: 7,820lb AUW: 10,600lb	Cruising speed: 115 mph Range 185 miles	Crew: 2 Passengers: 13
Bristol Britannia 102	Four 3,870 ehp Bristol Proteus 705	Wing span: 142ft 3in Length: 114ft 0in Height: 36ft 8in Wing area: 2,075 sq ft	Empty: 86,400lb AUW: 155,000lb	Cruising speed: 362 mph Range: 2,740 miles with max load	Crew: 3 Passengers: 83
Bristol Britannia 312	Four 4,120 ehp Bristol Proteus 761	Wing span: 142ft 3in Length: 124ft 3in Height: 36ft 8in Wing area: 2,075 sq ft	Empty: 88,000lb AUW: 180,000lb	Cruising speed: 355 mph Range: 4,100 miles with max load	Crew: 3-5 Passengers: 133
Saro Princess	Ten 3,780 ehp Bristol Proteus 600	Wing span: 219ft 6in Length: 148ft 0in Height: 55ft 9in	Empty: 191,000lb AUW: 330,000lb	Cruising speed: 360 mph Range: 5,270 miles	Crew: 3 Passengers: 200
Scottish Aviation Twin Pioneer 2	Two 600 hp Pratt & Whitney Wasp R-1340	Wing span: 76ft 6in Length: 45ft 3in Height: 12ft 3in Wing area: 670 sq ft	Empty: 10,900lb AUW: 14,000lb	Max speed: 187 mph Cruising speed: 122 mph Range: 670 miles	Crew: 2 Passengers: 16
Fairey Rotodyne	Two 5,250 ehp Rolls-Royce Tyne	Rotor dia: 104ft 0in Length: 64ft 6in Wing span: 56ft 6in Height: 23ft 2in	AUW: 53,500lb	Cruising speed: 200 mph Range: 650 miles	Crew: 2 Passengers: 54-70
Handley Page Dart Herald 200	Two 2,105 ehp Rolls-Royce Dart 527	Wing span: 94ft 9in Length: 75ft 6in Height: 24ft 0in Wing area: 886 sq ft	Empty: 24,960lb AUW: 43,000lb	Cruising speed: 275 mph Range: 1,760 miles	Crew: 2 Passengers: 56
Westland Widgeon	One 520 hp Alvis Leonides 521/2	Rotor dia: 49ft 2in Length: 57ft 8in Height: 13ft 2¾in	Empty: 4,322lb AUW: 5,900lb	Max speed: 110 mph Cruising speed: 81 mph Range: 310 miles	Crew: 1 Passengers: 4
Edgar Percival EP.9	One 270 hp Lycoming GO-480-B1.B	Wing span: 43ft 6in Length: 29ft 6in Height: 8ft 9in Wing area: 227.5 sq ft	Empty: 2,010lb AUW: 3,550lb	Max speed: 146 mph Cruising speed: 128 mph Range: 580 miles	Crew: 1-2 Passengers: 4-5
Vickers Vanguard 952	Four 5,545 ehp Rolls-Royce Tyne 512	Wing span: 118ft 7in Length: 122ft 10½in Height: 34ft 11in Wing area: 1,529 sq ft	Empty: 82,500lb AUW: 146,500lb	Cruising speed: 425 mph Range: 1,830 miles	Crew: 3-4 Passengers: 139
Hawker Siddeley HS.650 Argosy Series 200	Four 2,230 ehp Rolls-Royce Dart 532/1	Wing span: 115ft 0in Length: 86ft 9in Height: 29ft 3in Wing area: 1,458 sq ft	Empty: 48,830lb AUW: 93,000lb	Cruising speed: 280 mph Range: 1,850 miles	Crew: 2-3 Passengers: 89
BAe 748 Series 2A	Two 2,280 ehp Rolls-Royce Dart 532-2L	Wing span: 98ft 6in Length: 67ft 0in Height: 24ft 10in Wing area: 811 sq ft	Empty: 26,000lb AUW: 44,495lb	Cruising speed: 278 mph Range: 1,840 miles	Crew: 2 Passengers: 40-62

Type	Powerplant	Dimensions	Weights	Performance	Accommodation
Aviation Traders ATL.98 Carvair	Four 1,450 hp Pratt & Whitney Twin Wasp R-2000-7M2	Wing span: 117ft 6in Length: 102ft 7in Height: 29ft 10 in Wing area: 1,457 sq ft	Empty: 40,855lb AUW: 73,800lb	Max speed: 250 mph Cruising speed: 195 mph Range: 1,700 miles	Crew: 2-3 Passengers: 25 plus 5 cars
Beagle 206 Series 2	Two 340 hp Rolls-Royce Continental GTSIO-520C	Wing span: 45ft 9½in Length: 33ft 8in Height: 11ft 4in Wing area: 214 sq ft	Empty: 4,800lb AUW: 7,499lb	Max speed: 258 mph Cruising speed: 218 mph Range: 1,620 miles	Crew: 1 Passengers: 4-7
Vickers VC10	Four 21,000lb st Rolls-Royce Conway 540	Wing span: 146ft 2in Length: 158ft 8in Height: 39ft 6in Wing area: 2,932 sq ft	Empty: 139,505lb AUW: 312,000lb	Cruising speed: 568 mph Range: 6,725 miles	Crew: 3 Passengers: up to 151
Vickers Super VC10	Four 22,500lb st Rolls-Royce Conway 550	Wing span: 146ft 2in Length: 171ft 8in Height: 39ft 6in Wing area: 2,932 sq ft	Empty: 146,962lb AUW: 335,000lb	Cruising speed: 550 mph Range: 7,190 miles	Crew: 3-5 Passengers: 174
Hawker Siddeley Trident 2E	Three 11,930lb st Rolls-Royce Spey 512	Wing span: 98ft 10in Length: 114ft 9in Height: 27ft 0in Wing area: 1,456 sq ft	Empty: 73,800lb AUW: 142,500lb	Cruising speed: 590 mph Range: 2,700 miles	Crew: 3 Passengers: 149
Hawker Siddeley Trident 3B	Three 11,930lb st Rolls-Royce Spey 512 and one 5,250lb st Rolls-Royce RB.162	Wing span: 98ft 0in Length: 131ft 2in Height: 28ft 3in Wing area: 1,493 sq ft	Empty: 81,250lb AUW: 150,000lb	Cruising speed: 550 mph Range: 2,235 miles	Crew: 3 Passengers: up to 179
BAe 125 Series 400	Two 3,600lb st Bristol Siddeley Viper 522	Wing span: 47ft 0in Length: 47ft 5in Height: 16ft 6in Wing area: 353 sq ft	Empty: 11,275lb AUW: 23,300lb	Max cruising speed: 510 mph Econ cruising speed: 450 mph Max range: 1,940 miles	Crew: 2 Passengers: 7-12
Shorts Skyvan 3	Two 715 shp Garrett-AiResearch TPE331-201	Wing span: 64ft 11in Length: 40ft 1in Height: 15ft 1in Wing area: 373 sq ft	Empty: 7,344lb AUW: 12,500lb	Max speed: 250 mph Cruising speed: 195 mph Range: 694 miles	Crew: 1-2 Passengers: 19
BAe One-Eleven 400	Two 11,400lb st Rolls-Royce Spey 511	Wing span: 88ft 6in Length: 93ft 6in Height: 24ft 6in Wing area: 1,003 sq ft	Empty: 49,587lb AUW: 87,000lb	Cruising speed: 548 mph Range: 1,420 miles	Crew: 2 Passengers: 89
BAe One-Eleven 500	Two 12,000lb st Rolls-Royce Spey 512	Wing span: 93ft 6in Length: 107ft 0in Height: 24ft 6in Wing area: 1,031 sq ft	Empty: 54,595lb AUW: 98,000lb	Cruising speed: 540 mph Range: 1,420 miles	Crew: 2 Passengers: 97-109
Britten-Norman BN-2A Islander	Two 300 hp Lycoming IO-540-K1B5	Wing span: 49ft 0in Length: 35ft 8in Height: 13ft 8in Wing area: 325 sq ft	Empty: 3,500lb AUW: 6,000lb	Max speed: 168 mph Cruising speed: 150 mph Range: 810 miles	Crew: 1 Passengers: 9
Handley Page Jetstream	Two 840 hp Turboméca Astazou 14-CO1	Wing span: 52ft 0in Length: 47ft 1½in Height: 17ft 5½in Wing area: 270 sq ft	Empty: 8,450lb AUW: 12,500lb	Max speed: 282 mph Cruising speed: 250 mph Range: 1,900 miles	Crew: 2 Passengers: 12-16
BAe/Aérospatiale Concorde	Four 38,050lb st Rolls-Royce/Snecma Olympus 593	Wing span: 83ft 10in Length: 203ft 9in Height: 37ft 5in Wing area: 3,856 sq ft	Empty: 173,500lb AUW: 408,000lb	Max cruising speed: 1,354 mph (Mach 2.04) Max range: 4,090 miles	Crew: 3 Passengers: 128-144
Britten-Norman Trislander	Three 260 hp Lycoming O-540-E4C5	Wing span: 53ft 0in Length: 49ft 3in Height: 14ft 2in Wing area: 337 sq ft	Empty: 5,843lb AUW: 10,000lb	Max speed: 180 mph at S/L Cruising speed: 166 mph Range: 1,000 miles	Crew: 1-2 Passengers: 16
Shorts 330	Two 1,120 shp Pratt & Whitney PT6A-45A	Wing span: 74ft 8in Length: 58ft 0½in Height: 16ft 3in Wing area: 453 sq ft	Empty: 14,410lb AUW: 22,400lb	Max cruising speed: 227 mph Econ cruising speed: 184 mph Range: 506 miles	Crew: 2 Passengers: 30

Photograph Credits

Index